D0937877

GLEIM® | Aviation

SEVENTH
EDITION

PRIVATE PILOT
Syllabus

by
Irvin N. Gleim, Ph.D., CFII
and
Garrett W. Gleim, CFII

ABOUT THE AUTHORS

Irvin N. Gleim earned his private pilot certificate in 1965 from the Institute of Aviation at the University of Illinois, where he subsequently received his Ph.D. He is a commercial pilot and flight instructor (instrument) with multi-engine and seaplane ratings and is a member of the Aircraft Owners and Pilots Association, American Bonanza Society, Civil Air Patrol, Experimental Aircraft Association, National Association of Flight Instructors, and Seaplane Pilots Association. He is the author of flight maneuvers and practical test prep books for the sport, private, instrument, commercial, and flight instructor certificates/ratings and the author of study guides for the remote, sport, private/recreational, instrument, commercial, flight/ground instructor, fundamentals of instructing, airline transport pilot, and flight engineer FAA knowledge tests. Three additional pilot training books are *Pilot Handbook*, *Aviation Weather and Weather Services*, and *FAR/AIM*.

Dr. Gleim has also written articles for professional accounting and business law journals and is the author of widely used review manuals for the CIA (Certified Internal Auditor) exam, the CMA (Certified Management Accountant) exam, the CPA (Certified Public Accountant) exam, and the EA (IRS Enrolled Agent) exam. He is Professor Emeritus, Fisher School of Accounting, University of Florida, and is a CFM, CIA, CMA, and CPA.

Garrett W. Gleim earned his private pilot certificate in 1997 in a Piper Super Cub. He is a commercial pilot (single- and multi-engine), ground instructor (advanced and instrument), and flight instructor (instrument and multi-engine), and he is a member of the Aircraft Owners and Pilots Association, the National Association of Flight Instructors, and the Society of Aviation and Flight Educators. He is the author of study guides for the remote, sport, private/recreational, instrument, commercial, flight/ground instructor, fundamentals of instructing, and airline transport pilot FAA knowledge tests. He received a Bachelor of Science in Economics from The Wharton School, University of Pennsylvania. Mr. Gleim is also a CPA.

Gleim Publications, Inc.
PO Box 12848
Gainesville, Florida 32604

(352) 375-0772
(800) 87-GLEIM or (800) 874-5346

www.GleimAviation.com
aviationteam@gleim.com

For updates to the first printing of the seventh edition of
Private Pilot Syllabus

Go To: www.GleimAviation.com/updates

Or: Email update@gleim.com with **PPSYL 7-1**
in the subject line. You will receive our current
update as a reply.

Updates are available until the next edition is published.

ISSN 1097-1785
ISBN 978-1-61854-425-4

This edition is copyright © 2020 by Gleim Publications, Inc. Portions of this manuscript are taken from previous editions copyright © 1998-2016 by Gleim Publications, Inc.

First Printing: December 2020

ALL RIGHTS RESERVED. No part of this material may be reproduced in any form whatsoever without express written permission from Gleim Publications, Inc. Reward is offered for information exposing violators. Contact copyright@gleim.com.

Let Us Know!

This syllabus is designed specifically for student pilots who aspire to obtain the private pilot certificate.

Please submit any corrections and suggestions for subsequent editions to the authors at www.GleimAviation.com/Questions.

Also, please bring Gleim books to the attention of flight instructors, fixed-base operators, and others interested in flying. Wide distribution of this series of books and increased interest in flying depend on your assistance and good word. Thank you.

Environmental Statement -- This book is printed on recycled paper sourced from suppliers certified using sustainable forestry management processes.

If necessary, we will develop an UPDATE for *Private Pilot Syllabus*. Visit our website or email update@gleim.com for the latest updates. Updates for this edition will be available until the next edition is published. To continue providing our customers with first-rate service, we request that technical questions about our materials be sent to us via www.GleimAviation.com/Questions. We will give each question thorough consideration and a prompt response. Questions concerning orders, prices, shipments, or payments will be handled via telephone by our competent and courteous customer service staff.

TABLE OF CONTENTS

IF FOUND, PLEASE CONTACT

Pilot Name _____

Address _____

_____

_____

Telephone # _____

Email _____

PREFACE

Thank you for choosing Gleim. Our training materials (books, software, audios, and online) are intuitively appealing and thus very effective in transferring knowledge to you. The Gleim system saves you time, money, and frustration vs. other aviation training programs.

This syllabus will facilitate your studies and training for your private pilot certificate.

1. Please read the following Introduction carefully.

2. The "Lesson Sequence and Times" section on pages 10 and 11 shows ground lessons being completed as you complete flight lessons. We encourage you to work ahead in your ground lessons and begin them (and even complete them) prior to beginning your flight training.

3. Completion of your flight training in 35 or 40 hours is achievable; however, most individuals take 50+ hours. Thus, some flight lessons will take more than one flight to complete.

 The **objective** is to develop "ACS level" proficiency as quickly as possible. "ACS level" means you can perform at the level required by the FAA's Airman Certification Standards.

4. Homework consists of reading and/or studying your Gleim reference books or online courseware and the Pilot's Operating Handbook or Operating Limitations for your airplane. Each flight lesson also directs you to review topics and material studied for previous lessons. The Gleim *FAR/AIM* book is for reference.

 Why is the GLEIM SYSTEM different? It focuses on successful completion, as quickly and as easily as possible. The requirements for earning your private pilot certificate are listed beginning on page 2. This syllabus facilitates your flight training so you achieve an "ACS level" of proficiency on the 45 FAA "tasks" as quickly as possible!

 GO FOR IT! Start studying for your FAA knowledge test today. Refer to *Private Pilot FAA Knowledge Test Prep* and *Pilot Handbook*. Start studying for your FAA practical test by reading *Private Pilot Flight Maneuvers and Practical Test Prep*.

 We have an easy-to-follow and easy-to-complete study system. From the very start, we want you to focus on success. This means answering over 80% of the FAA knowledge test questions correctly AND being able to explain and demonstrate the 45 FAA practical test tasks to your CFI at "ACS level" proficiency for airplane single-engine land.

Enjoy Flying Safely!

Irvin N. Gleim
Garrett W. Gleim

December 2020

INTRODUCTION

This syllabus is a step-by-step lesson plan for your private pilot training. The basic requirements of the Federal Aviation Administration (FAA) private pilot certificate are discussed on the following pages. This syllabus is intended to be used in conjunction with the current edition of the following four Gleim books:

Private Pilot FAA Knowledge Test Prep
Private Pilot Flight Maneuvers and Practical Test Prep
Private Pilot ACS & Oral Exam Guide
Pilot Handbook
FAR/AIM

Your flight instructor will fill out the companion Flight Training Record as you complete each flight lesson. The Flight Training Record should remain at the flight school as a record of your progress.

WHAT ELSE DO YOU NEED?

If you purchased this syllabus as part of the Gleim **Private Pilot Kit**, you will need to purchase a local sectional chart and a Chart Supplement appropriate to your region. They are published every 6 months and 56 days, respectively. You will need a current copy of each for your FAA practical test. Gleim does not include these publications in your kit because there are 37 different sectional charts and seven different Chart Supplements for the conterminous U.S.

Additionally, you will need to purchase a copy of the Pilot's Operating Handbook and/or Airplane Flight Manual (POH/AFM) (or a Pilot Information Manual) for the make and model of your training airplane. Alternatively, you may make a photocopy if a POH/AFM is not available for purchase.

REQUIREMENTS FOR PRIVATE PILOT CERTIFICATE

There are a number of requirements to earn your private pilot certificate. The final step is your FAA practical test, which will be conducted by an appropriate FAA evaluator. Your practical test will consist of an approximately 1-hour oral exam followed by a 1- to 2-hour flight test. You will be well prepared for your practical test by your CFI and your Gleim pilot training materials. In addition, you must meet the following requirements:

1. Obtain an FAA medical certificate or operate under BasicMed.

    a. Your medical exam will be conducted by an FAA-designated aviation medical examiner (AME).

    b. Ask your CFI or call your local flight school for the names and telephone numbers of the AMEs in your area, or visit www.faa.gov/pilots/amelocator for a listing of AMEs by country, county, city, zip code, or last name.

    c. Use the FAA's MedXPress system to digitally fill out and submit your medical application before arriving at your appointment with the AME.

        1) Access MedXPress at https://medxpress.faa.gov.

    d. BasicMed allows a pilot to conduct certain VFR and IFR operations using a U.S. driver's license instead of a medical certificate as long as the pilot meets the conditions found in 14 CFR 61.23 and 14 CFR Part 68.

2. Obtain an FAA student pilot certificate. A student pilot certificate will be issued by a Certificated Flight Instructor (CFI), Airmen Certification Representative (ACR), aviation safety inspector (ASI), or designated pilot examiner (DPE).

    a. Contact a CFI, ACR, ASI, or DPE to schedule an appointment to have your completed and signed FAA Form 8710-1, *Airman Certificate and/or Rating Application*, processed and submitted to the FAA's Airman Certification Branch. The web address is https://iacra.faa.gov.

        1) Make sure to bring the following documents to your appointment:

            a) Your completed and signed application

            b) An acceptable form of photo identification

            c) Documents necessary to verify citizenship, such as a U.S. birth certificate or U.S. passport

    b. Your instructor or FBO will be able to recommend the most convenient way of obtaining a student pilot certificate.

    c. Additionally, you may contact your regional FAA Flight Standards District Office (FSDO) and ask for the contact information of ASIs and DPEs in your area. To find the phone numbers of your regional FAA FSDO, visit the FAA's FSDO website at www.faa.gov/about/office_org/field_offices/fsdo.

3. Pass your FAA pilot knowledge test, which consists of 60 multiple-choice questions and is administered at an FAA-designated computer testing center. You will attend one of hundreds of computer testing centers after you have prepared for your test. Everything you need to prepare for your FAA pilot knowledge test is in your Gleim *Private Pilot FAA Knowledge Test Prep* and *Pilot Handbook* books. Gleim **FAA Test Prep Online** will facilitate your study. Use the Gleim **Online Ground School** for convenient, complete knowledge test study from any computer with Internet access. We have estimated 35 hours for complete preparation for your pilot knowledge test. You may turn to page 8 for instructions on how to begin at any time.

4. Undertake flight training as described in Lessons 1 through 26 beginning on page 33. Many of the lessons will require more than one flight to complete. We also have provided space for your instructor to record extra flights within each lesson as needed to make you comfortable and proficient.

5.   Pass your FAA practical test. See ***Private Pilot Flight Maneuvers and Practical Test Prep***.

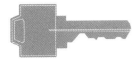 The KEY TO SUCCESS in your flight training, which also minimizes cost and frustration, is your study and preparation at home before flying with your flight instructor. The more you know about flying, flight training, and each flight lesson, the better you will do.

The importance of home study certainly applies to piloting. You should arrive at each of your flight lessons ready to fly. Your flight training will be completed faster, you will save money, and you will have a far more productive and enjoyable experience.

It's fun to be successful! Be overly prepared before you get to the airport for each flight lesson.

PART 141 VS. PART 61 SCHOOLS

The Code of Federal Regulations, Title 14: Aeronautics and Space (14 CFR) lists the requirements to obtain your private pilot certificate. Flight schools can conduct your training by following either 14 CFR Part 141 or 14 CFR Part 61.

A Part 141 flight school is issued a pilot school certificate by the FAA after applying to the FAA and meeting certain requirements. A Part 141 flight school's syllabus is approved by the FAA during this certification process. Thus, if you are using the Gleim ***Private Pilot Syllabus*** in a Part 141 flight school, it must be used in your training.

The majority of flight schools, and flight instructors not associated with a flight school, provide the required training as specified under Part 61.

The major difference between Part 141 and Part 61 training is in the minimum amount of total flight time and solo flight time. Generally, a Part 141 school is more regimented than a Part 61 school; thus, the FAA set the minimum flight time at 35 hours under Part 141 and 40 hours under Part 61. However, the 35- vs. 40-hour minimum requirement often is not relevant because most people require additional time to complete their private pilot training.

You should select a flight instructor and/or flight school that you are comfortable with rather than being concerned with whether the training is conducted under Part 141 or Part 61. This syllabus meets the requirements for either Part 141 or Part 61.

The Gleim syllabus has been reviewed by the FAA in Washington, D.C., and found to adequately meet the requirements of a syllabus under Part 141 or Part 61, as appropriate. However, the final approval of a syllabus for use under Part 141 must come from the responsible Flight Standards office. Thus, the Gleim ***Private Pilot Syllabus*** can be used by any Part 141 school with minimum effort.

If a Part 141 school cannot or will not use this syllabus, consider finding another Part 141 or Part 61 school for your training OR please call Gleim at (800) 874-5346 if you have questions or problems.

PART 141 STUDENT INFORMATION

Enrollment Prerequisites

A student must hold a student, sport, or recreational pilot certificate before enrolling in the solo flight phase of the private pilot certification course. The student must be able to obtain at least a third-class medical certificate or operate under the provisions of BasicMed (14 CFR 61.113).

Solo Flight Requirements

Before a student can fly solo, (s)he must complete the specified training, pass a presolo knowledge test, and receive the required logbook endorsements from his or her flight instructor.

Graduation Requirements

The student must complete the training specified in this syllabus, with a minimum of 35 hours of ground training in the specified aeronautical knowledge areas and a minimum of 35 hours of flight training (20 hours of dual and 5 hours of solo). These requirements are reflected in the Gleim Flight Training Syllabus beginning on page 29.

Stage Checks

The student must score a minimum of 80% on the stage one and two knowledge tests at the completion of each stage in the ground training syllabus and must score a minimum of 80% on a comprehensive end-of-course knowledge test at the conclusion of the training.

The student must satisfactorily complete a stage one and two flight check at the completion of each stage of the flight training syllabus. And finally, the student must satisfactorily complete the end-of-course flight test.

Credit for Previous Training

The student may be given the following credit toward this private pilot certification course for previous pilot experience and knowledge [14 CFR Sec. 141.77(c)]:

1.   If the credit is based on a Part 141 training course, the credit may be 50% of the requirements for this course.

2.   If the credit is based on a Part 61 course, the credit cannot exceed 25% of the requirements for this course.

The receiving school will determine the amount of course credit to be given, based on a proficiency test, a knowledge test, or both.

EXPLANATION OF *PRIVATE PILOT TRAINING RECORD*

Also available separately from this syllabus is the Gleim *Private Pilot Training Record*. This record is provided for flight schools that conduct training under 14 CFR Part 141, which requires that detailed training records be maintained for each student. When properly completed, the training record booklet will meet the training record requirements of Part 141.

Training Record Elements

The training record consists of three main sections:

-   The front cover contains student personal information and information about the training course.
-   The back cover serves as a ground training record and student flight evaluation record.
-   The inside of the booklet consists of a flight training record, specific flight lesson records, and a separate record of instructor endorsements.

Using the Private Pilot Training Record

Front Cover: The front cover of the training record should be filled out by the student, his or her flight instructor, and the chief flight instructor at the time of enrollment. Spaces provided to record credit awarded for previous ground and flight training should be completed by the chief instructor. The chief instructor also should complete the enrollment certificate (found on page 87 of this syllabus) and place it in the training record.

At the completion of training, the chief instructor should complete the information on the front cover, as appropriate (e.g., graduation, transfer, or termination). If the student has graduated, the graduation certificate (found on page 89 of this syllabus) should be completed and placed in the training record.

Back Cover: The ground training record should be filled out by the instructor after each ground lesson is completed, regardless of whether ground training is being conducted formally or as a self-study program. The time spent and date of completion should be noted and the record initialed by both the student and the instructor.

The stage and end-of-course test records should be filled out by the instructor after each stage and end-of-course test has been taken by the student, graded, and reviewed with the instructor. The date of the test, the result, and the date of the review should be noted. The record should then be initialed by the student and signed by the instructor. Each stage and end-of-course test answer sheet should also be placed in the training record.

The student flight evaluation records should be filled out by the instructor following the presolo knowledge test and evaluation and by the chief instructor after each stage check. The date and result of the end-of-course test should be noted and the record initialed by the student and signed by the instructor or chief instructor (the chief instructor must sign the record for each stage check).

Inside: The flight training record consists of three parts:

1. The record of instructor endorsements is a record of information related to each flight instructor endorsement that is pertinent to the course of training,

2. The flight training record is a chronological record of each training flight that is made during the course, and

3. The flight lesson record is an itemized record of the student's performance on the lesson items listed in each specific flight lesson.

AIRPLANE(S) AND LOCAL AIRPORT(S) WORKSHEETS

The airplane(s) worksheet on page 6 is to be used as a study reference of fuel, oil, and airspeeds for the airplane(s) you may use during your training. The local airport(s) worksheet (on page 7) is to be used as a study reference of elevation, radio frequencies, traffic pattern direction, and runway lengths at your primary airport and any other local airports you may use during your training.

AIRPLANE(S) WORKSHEET

N-number

Make & Model

Max. Ramp Wt.

Fuel Capacity

Min. Fuel for Flight

Oil Capacity

Min. Oil for Flight

V_{S0}

V_{S1}

V_R

V_X

V_Y

V_{FE}

V_A

V_{NO}

V_{NE}

Best Glide

LOCAL AIRPORT(S) WORKSHEET

Airport Name	_____	_____	_____	_____	_____
Identifier	_____	_____	_____	_____	_____
Elevation	_____	_____	_____	_____	_____
ATIS	_____	_____	_____	_____	_____
Ground	_____	_____	_____	_____	_____
Tower	_____	_____	_____	_____	_____
UNICOM	_____	_____	_____	_____	_____
Runway	_____	_____	_____	_____	_____
Length	_____	_____	_____	_____	_____
Traffic Pattern	Left or Right	Left or Right	Left or Right	Left or Right	Left or Right
Obstructions	_____	_____	_____	_____	_____
Runway	_____	_____	_____	_____	_____
Length	_____	_____	_____	_____	_____
Traffic Pattern	Left or Right	Left or Right	Left or Right	Left or Right	Left or Right
Obstructions	_____	_____	_____	_____	_____
Runway	_____	_____	_____	_____	_____
Length	_____	_____	_____	_____	_____
Traffic Pattern	Left or Right	Left or Right	Left or Right	Left or Right	Left or Right
Obstructions	_____	_____	_____	_____	_____
Runway	_____	_____	_____	_____	_____
Length	_____	_____	_____	_____	_____
Traffic Pattern	Left or Right	Left or Right	Left or Right	Left or Right	Left or Right
Obstructions	_____	_____	_____	_____	_____
Traffic Pattern Altitude	_____	_____	_____	_____	_____

GLEIM *PRIVATE PILOT SYLLABUS*

This syllabus consists of a ground training syllabus and a flight training syllabus. The ground and flight training may be done separately or together as an integrated course of instruction.

This syllabus was constructed using the building-block progression of learning, in which the student is required to perform each simple task correctly before a more complex task is introduced. This method will promote the formation of correct habit patterns from the beginning.

Ground Training Syllabus

The ground training syllabus contains 11 lessons, which are divided into two stages. The ground training syllabus meets the training requirements of 14 CFR Part 61 and Appendix B to 14 CFR Part 141. The ground training can be conducted concurrently with the flight training, with the ground lessons completed in order as outlined in the lesson matrix, beginning on page 10. Ground training may also be conducted as part of a formal ground school or as a home-study program.

It is recommended that the lessons be completed in sequence, but the syllabus is flexible enough to meet the needs of an individual student or of a particular training environment. When departing from the sequence, the instructor is responsible for considering the blocks of learning affected.

Each ground lesson involves studying the appropriate study unit in the Gleim *Pilot Handbook*. After each reading assignment is completed, you need to answer the questions in the appropriate study unit in the Gleim *Private Pilot FAA Knowledge Test Prep* book and review incorrect responses with your instructor.

Alternatively, the Gleim **FAA Test Prep Online** can be used to answer the questions at the end of each ground lesson. Our software contains the FAA figures and outlines in addition to the questions.

FAA Test Prep Online allows you to select either STUDY MODE or TEST MODE. In STUDY MODE, the software provides you with an immediate explanation of each answer you choose (correct or incorrect). You design each study lesson by choosing the conditions. In TEST MODE, the software can emulate the operation of the FAA-approved computer testing centers. Thus, you will have a complete understanding of exactly how to take an FAA private pilot airman knowledge test before you go to a computer testing center. When you finish your test, you can study the questions missed and access answer explanations.

A third option for ground study is the Gleim **Online Ground School (OGS)**. OGS uses a similar approach to a traditional ground school in that each lesson is presented in order and divided into stages, per the syllabus book. The course contains audiovisual presentations, detailed study material, and quizzes for maximum retention of the information covered.

Because OGS is a self-study program delivered via the Internet, the classroom is always open, so you can study as it fits in to your schedule. When you complete the program and pass the end-of-course knowledge test, an endorsement will be provided to you that will enable you to take the FAA knowledge test at a testing center. This feature makes OGS especially valuable to those users electing to complete their ground training before beginning flight training.

At the end of each stage, you are required to complete the stage knowledge test before proceeding to the next stage. The end-of-course knowledge test is completed after the stage two knowledge test. Shortly after the end-of-course test, you should take the FAA private pilot airman knowledge test. The stage knowledge tests in the ground syllabus will refer you to FAA figures found after the end-of-course knowledge test in this syllabus.

If this ground training is home study, we recommend that you complete the syllabus as quickly as possible and pass the FAA private pilot knowledge test so you will have more time to prepare for your flight lessons.

Flight Training Syllabus

The Part 141 flight training syllabus contains 26 lessons (28 lessons if Part 61), which are divided into two stages. It is recommended that each lesson be completed in sequential order.

Stage One of the flight training syllabus is designed to provide the student with a foundation of good flying habits for his or her flying career. This stage ends with the student's first solo flight. During this stage, the student will become proficient in the knowledge, procedures, and maneuvers required for solo flight. Prior to the student's first solo flight, (s)he will complete the presolo knowledge test. The instructor is responsible for ensuring that the student meets the applicable requirements of 14 CFR 61.87, Solo Requirements for Student Pilots.

Stage Two is designed to provide the student with the knowledge and skills required for confident, repeated solo flight, including cross country navigation. This stage also addresses night-flying and preparation for the FAA private pilot practical test. Part 141 requires one solo cross-country flight of at least 100 NM, while Part 61 requires a total of 5 hours of solo cross-country flight time, with one flight of at least 150 NM. We have included two additional solo cross-country lessons to meet the Part 61 solo time requirements. These flights are optional and need not be performed if you are using this syllabus under Part 141.

Stage checks. Stage checks are designed to ensure that the student has acquired the necessary knowledge and skill. The stage one check (flight lesson 12) is to ensure that the student is competent for safe solo flight. The stage two check (flight lesson 25) is a cumulative review, and the end-of-course test (flight lesson 26) is a final check before issuing a Part 141 graduation certificate.

The chief flight instructor (Part 141) is responsible for ensuring that each student accomplishes the required stage checks and end-of-course test. The chief flight instructor may delegate authority for conducting stage checks and end-of-course test to the assistant chief flight instructor or a check instructor.

Stage checks will be used as a review by instructors training under Part 61 to ensure that the student has the appropriate knowledge and skills.

Sequence of a flight lesson. Each flight lesson will begin with a preflight briefing. During this time, the instructor should first answer any questions the student may have from the previous lesson. Next, the instructor will brief the student on the lesson content, including the objectives, maneuvers, expected student actions, and completion standards. The instructor should discuss the knowledge, risk management, and skill elements appropriate for the flight. In addition, during this briefing, the instructor will evaluate the student's preparation for the lesson. Prior to a solo flight, the instructor must review with the student the maneuvers to be done, the objective of the lesson, and the completion standards.

During the flight portion of the lesson, the instructor should begin with those maneuvers listed as review before introducing new maneuvers. The time required for each lesson will vary depending on the airport and the location of the training areas.

At the end of each lesson, the instructor will conduct a postflight critique and a preview of the next lesson. This time should be used to review the good points during the lesson, to identify and explain fully any problem areas, and to discuss how to correct the problems. The debrief should include a self-assessment by the student, any questions the student may have, and whether completion standards were met.

The length of the preflight briefing and postflight critique will vary with each student and with his or her degree of preparedness for the lesson.

Student preparation. The key to minimizing frustration and costs is preparation. You should budget an average of 2 to 4 hours of home study prior to each flight lesson. Learning will be easier when you are fully prepared so that your instructor can maximize the time spent in flight training.

PRIVATE PILOT SYLLABUS GROUND AND FLIGHT LESSON SEQUENCE AND TIMES

The following table lists the sequence of the flight and ground lessons and the minimum time for each lesson. The times listed are for instructor/student guidance only and are not meant to be mandatory times. These times will ensure that the minimum time requirements for aeronautical knowledge and flight training are in compliance either with 14 CFR Part 141, Appendix B, Private Pilot Certification Course, or with 14 CFR Part 61.

Each training flight (solo and dual) must include a preflight briefing and a postflight critique of the student's performance by the instructor. This time will be entered into the logbook as "ground training."

LESSON	Page	Flight Training (Dual)	Solo/ PIC	Dual Cross-Country	Solo Cross-Country	Night	Instrument	Aeronautical Knowledge Training
STAGE ONE								
Flight 1: Introduction to Flight	33	1.0						
Ground 1: Airplanes and Aerodynamics	15							3.0
Flight 2: Four Fundamentals of Flight	34	1.0						
Ground 2: Airplane Instruments, Engines, and Systems	16							3.0
Flight 3: Basic Instrument Maneuvers	35	1.5					0.5	
Ground 3: Airports, Air Traffic Control, and Airspace	17							3.0
Flight 4: Slow Flight and Stalls	36	1.5						
Ground 4: Federal Aviation Regulations	18							3.0
Flight 5: Emergency Operations	37	1.5						
Flight 6: Performance Maneuvers	38	1.5						
Flight 7: Review	39	1.5						
Ground 5: Airplane Performance and Weight and Balance	19							3.0
Flight 8: Go-Around and Forward Slip to a Landing	40	1.5						
Flight 9: Presolo Review	41	1.5					0.3	
Flight 10: Presolo Review	42	1.5						
Flight Presolo Knowledge Test	63							
Flight 11: First Solo	43	0.5	0.5					
Ground Stage One Knowledge Test	20/67							1.0
Flight 12: Stage One Check	44	1.0					0.2	

| LESSON | Page | Flight | | | | | | Ground |
		Flight Training (Dual)	Solo/ PIC	Dual Cross-Country	Solo Cross-Country	Night	Instrument	Aeronautical Knowledge Training
STAGE TWO								
Ground 6: Aeromedical Factors and Aeronautical Decision Making	21							2.0
Flight 13: Second Solo	46	1.0	0.5					
Ground 7: Aviation Weather	22							3.0
Flight 14: Short-Field and Soft-Field Takeoffs and Landings	47	1.5						
Ground 8: Aviation Weather Services	23							2.5
Flight 15: Solo Maneuvers Review	48		1.0					
Ground 9: Navigation: Charts and Publications	24							3.0
Ground 10: Navigation Systems	25							2.5
Flight 16: Navigation Systems	49	1.5					0.5	
Ground 11: Cross-Country Flight Planning	26							2.5
Flight 17: Dual Cross-Country	50	1.7		1.7				
Ground Stage Two Knowledge Test	27/70							1.0
Flight 18: Night Flight - Local	51	1.3				1.3	0.3	
Ground End-of-Course Knowledge Test	27/72							2.5
Flight 19: Night Cross-Country	52	1.7		1.7		1.7	0.4	
Flight 20*/**: Solo Cross-Country (Part 61/141)	53		2.0*/**		2.0*/**			
Flight 20A**: Solo Cross-Country (Part 61)	54		3.0**		3.0**			
Flight 20B**: Solo Cross-Country or Local Flight (Part 61)	55		2.0**		2.0**			
Flight 21: Maneuvers Review	56	1.2						
Flight 22: Solo Practice	57		0.8					
Flight 23: Maneuvers Review	58	1.2					0.3	
Flight 24: Solo Practice	59		0.8					
Flight 25: Stage Two Check	60	1.3					0.2	
Flight 26: End of Course Test	61	1.5					0.3	
Part 141 TOTALS		29.4	5.6*	3.4	2.0*	3.0	3.0	35.0
Part 61 TOTALS		29.4	10.6**	3.4	7.0**	3.0	3.0	35.0
		Total Times						

*Part 141 requires one solo cross-country flight of at least 100 NM total distance with landings at a minimum of three points; one segment of the flight must have a straight-line distance of at least 50 NM between the takeoff and landing locations. Since no minimum time is required, we have allocated 2 hours for this flight in Flight 20.

**Part 61 requires a minimum of 5 hours of solo cross-country flight time, including one flight of at least 150 NM total distance with landings at a minimum of three points; one segment of the flight must have a straight-line distance of at least 50 NM between the takeoff and landing locations. Flights 20, 20A, and 20B are used to meet these solo cross-country and total solo time requirements. Since only 5 hours of solo cross-country is needed, Lesson 20B may be replaced with 2.0 hours of local solo practice.

USE OF FLIGHT SIMULATION TRAINING DEVICES (FSTDs) AND AVIATION TRAINING DEVICES (ATDs)

FSTDs include full flight simulators (FFSs) and flight training devices (FTDs). A Part 141 approved private pilot course may include training in a full flight simulator or flight training device, provided it is representative of the aircraft for which the course is approved, meets the requirements of 14 CFR 141.41(a), and the training is given by an authorized instructor. Training in a full flight simulator may be credited for a maximum of 20% of the total flight training hour requirements of the approved course (20% × 35 hours = 7.0 hours). Training in a flight training device may be credited for a maximum of 15% of the total flight training hour requirements of the approved course (15% × 35 hours = 5.25 hours). Training in a combination of full flight simulators and flight training devices may be credited for a maximum of 20% of the total flight training hour requirements of the approved course; however, credit for training in a flight training device cannot exceed the 15% limitation.

Part 61 allows a maximum of 2.5 hours of training in a FSTD. The device must be qualified and approved by 14 CFR Part 60 and the training provided by an authorized instructor.

ATDs include basic aviation training devices (BATDs) and advanced aviation training devices (AATDs). To credit time in an ATD it must be FAA-approved and the time must be provided by an authorized instructor. AC 61-136B provides information and guidance for the use of ATDs.

Gleim X-Plane Flight Training Course

One method of efficient ground training is use of a home simulator. By practicing each lesson on the ground, your time in the airplane will be more effective. Off-the-shelf flight simulator software for use at home may not be approved for official flight training. However, structured practice can enhance your training by providing additional understanding and familiarization with maneuvers and procedures.

Although the flight time may not count toward your training, you will still gain valuable experience to build proficiency and confidence. This can ultimately save you a significant amount of expensive aircraft rental time.

PRIVATE PILOT
GROUND TRAINING SYLLABUS
AIRPLANE SINGLE-ENGINE LAND

GROUND TRAINING COURSE OBJECTIVES

The student will obtain the necessary aeronautical knowledge and meet the prerequisites specified in Appendix B to 14 CFR Part 141 (and 14 CFR 61.105) to successfully pass the private pilot knowledge test.

GROUND TRAINING COURSE COMPLETION STANDARDS

The student will demonstrate through stage knowledge tests and school records that (s)he meets the prerequisites specified in Appendix B to 14 CFR Part 141 (and 14 CFR 61.105) and has the aeronautical knowledge necessary to pass the private pilot knowledge test.

Lesson	Topic	Min. Time in Hours
	Stage One	
1	Airplanes and Aerodynamics	3.0
2	Airplane Instruments, Engines, and Systems	3.0
3	Airports, Air Traffic Control, and Airspace	3.0
4	Federal Aviation Regulations	3.0
5	Airplane Performance and Weight and Balance	3.0
	Stage One Knowledge Test	1.0
	Stage Two	
6	Aeromedical Factors and Aeronautical Decision Making (ADM)	2.0
7	Aviation Weather	3.0
8	Aviation Weather Services	2.5
9	Navigation: Charts and Publications	3.0
10	Navigation Systems	2.5
11	Cross-Country Flight Planning	2.5
	Stage Two Knowledge Test	1.0
	End-of-Course Knowledge Test	2.5
		35.0

STAGE ONE

Stage One Objective

To develop the student's knowledge of airplanes and the aerodynamic principles of flight. The student will learn about the operation of various airplane systems, airport operations, radio communication procedures, air traffic control (ATC) radar services, and the National Airspace System (NAS). Additionally, the student will become familiar with pertinent Federal Aviation Regulations (14 CFR) and the accident-reporting requirements of the National Transportation Safety Board (NTSB). Finally, the student will learn how to predict airplane performance and how to control the weight and balance of the airplane.

Stage One Completion Standards

Stage One will have been successfully completed when the student passes the Stage One knowledge test with a minimum passing grade of 80%.

GROUND LESSON 1: AIRPLANES AND AERODYNAMICS

Objective

To develop the student's knowledge of airplanes, the aerodynamics of flight, and airplane stability.

Text References

Pilot Handbook, Study Unit 1, "Airplanes and Aerodynamics"
Private Pilot FAA Knowledge Test Prep, Study Unit 1, "Airplanes and Aerodynamics"

Pilot Handbook Study Unit 1 Contents	*Private Pilot FAA Knowledge Test Prep* Study Unit 1 Contents
1.1 Definitions 1.2 The Airplane 1.3 Composite Construction 1.4 Axes of Rotation 1.5 Flight Controls and Control Surfaces 1.6 Forces Acting on the Airplane in Flight 1.7 Dynamics of the Airplane in Flight 1.8 Ground Effect 1.9 How Airplanes Turn 1.10 Torque (Left-Turning Tendency) 1.11 Airplane Stability 1.12 Loads and Load Factors 1.13 Stalls and Spins 1.14 Angle of Attack Indicators	1.1 Flight Controls 1.2 Aerodynamic Forces 1.3 Angle of Attack 1.4 Stalls 1.5 Spins 1.6 Ground Effect 1.7 Airplane Turn 1.8 Airplane Stability 1.9 Torque and P-Factor 1.10 Load Factor 1.11 Velocity Vs. G-Loads

Completion Standards

The lesson will have been successfully completed when the student answers the questions in Study Unit 1, "Airplanes and Aerodynamics," of *Private Pilot FAA Knowledge Test Prep*, FAA Test Prep Online, and/or Online Ground School with a minimum passing grade of 80%.

	Dates Studied	Date Completed
Pilot Handbook	—— —— —— —— ——	——
Private Pilot FAA Knowledge Test Prep	—— —— —— —— ——	——

Notes:

GROUND LESSON 2: AIRPLANE INSTRUMENTS, ENGINES, AND SYSTEMS

Objective

To develop the student's knowledge of airplane instruments, engines, and systems.

Text References

Pilot Handbook, Study Unit 2, "Airplane Instruments, Engines, and Systems"
Private Pilot FAA Knowledge Test Prep, Study Unit 2, "Airplane Instruments, Engines, and Systems"

Pilot Handbook Study Unit 2 Contents	*Private Pilot FAA Knowledge Test Prep* Study Unit 2 Contents
2.1 Pitot-Static System	2.1 Compass Turning Error
2.2 Altimeter	2.2 Pitot-Static System
2.3 Vertical Speed Indicator	2.3 Airspeed Indicator
2.4 Airspeed Indicator	2.4 Altimeter
2.5 Gyroscopic Flight Instruments	2.5 Types of Altitude
2.6 Turn Coordinator	2.6 Setting the Altimeter
2.7 Turn-and-Slip Indicator	2.7 Altimeter Errors
2.8 Attitude Indicator	2.8 Gyroscopic Instruments
2.9 Heading Indicator	2.9 Glass Cockpits
2.10 Magnetic Compass	2.10 Engine Temperature
2.11 Compass Errors	2.11 Constant-Speed Propeller
2.12 Glass Cockpit Instrumentation	2.12 Engine Ignition Systems
2.13 Powerplant	2.13 Carburetor Icing
2.14 How an Engine Operates	2.14 Carburetor Heat
2.15 Ignition System	2.15 Fuel/Air Mixture
2.16 Induction System	2.16 Abnormal Combustion
2.17 Fuel System	2.17 Aviation Fuel Practices
2.18 Oil System	2.18 Starting the Engine
2.19 Cooling System	2.19 Cold Weather – Attention
2.20 Propellers	2.20 Electrical System
2.21 Full Authority Digital Engine Control (FADEC)	
2.22 Electrical System	
2.23 Landing Gear System	
2.24 Environmental System	
2.25 Deice and Anti-Ice Systems	

Completion Standards

The lesson will have been successfully completed when the student answers the questions in Study Unit 2, "Airplane Instruments, Engines, and Systems," of *Private Pilot FAA Knowledge Test Prep*, FAA Test Prep Online, and/or Online Ground School with a minimum passing grade of 80%.

	Dates Studied	Date Completed
Pilot Handbook	____ ____ ____ ____ ____	____
Private Pilot FAA Knowledge Test Prep	____ ____ ____ ____ ____	____

Notes:

GROUND LESSON 3: AIRPORTS, AIR TRAFFIC CONTROL, AND AIRSPACE

Objective

To develop the student's knowledge of airports, wake turbulence and collision avoidance, radio communication procedures and phraseology, ATC radar services, and the National Airspace System.

Text References

Pilot Handbook, Study Unit 3, "Airports, Air Traffic Control, and Airspace"
Private Pilot FAA Knowledge Test Prep, Study Unit 3, "Airports, Air Traffic Control, and Airspace"

Pilot Handbook Study Unit 3 Contents	*Private Pilot FAA Knowledge Test Prep* Study Unit 3 Contents
3.1 Runway and Taxiway Markings 3.2 Airport Lighting 3.3 Visual Glideslope Indicators 3.4 Wind and Landing Direction Indicators and Segmented Circles 3.5 Airport Traffic Patterns 3.6 Land and Hold Short Operations (LAHSO) 3.7 Wake Turbulence 3.8 Collision Avoidance 3.9 Radio Communications and Phraseology 3.10 Airports without an Operating Control Tower 3.11 Automated Weather Reporting Systems 3.12 Airports with an Operating Control Tower 3.13 Automatic Terminal Information Service (ATIS) 3.14 Ground Control 3.15 Tower Control 3.16 Approach Control and Departure Control (for VFR Aircraft) 3.17 Clearance Delivery 3.18 Emergencies 3.19 Radio Failure Procedures 3.20 Emergency Locator Transmitter (ELT) 3.21 ATC Radar 3.22 Transponder Operation 3.23 Radar Services to VFR Aircraft 3.24 General Dimensions of Airspace 3.25 Controlled and Uncontrolled Airspace 3.26-3.31 Class A, B, C, D, E, and G Airspace 3.32 Special-Use Airspace 3.33 Other Airspace Areas 3.34 Special Flight Rules Areas 3.35 Next Generation Air Transportation System (NextGen)	3.1 Runway Markings 3.2 Taxiway and Destination Signs 3.3 Beacons and Taxiway Lights 3.4 Airport Traffic Patterns 3.5 Visual Approach Slope Indicators (VASI) 3.6 Wake Turbulence 3.7 Collision Avoidance 3.8 ATIS and ATC Communications 3.9 Airspace 3.10 Terminal Radar Programs 3.11 Transponders and Transponder Codes 3.12 Radio Phraseology 3.13 ATC Traffic Advisories 3.14 ATC Light Signals 3.15 ELTs and VHF/DF 3.16 Emergency Radio Frequency 3.17 Land and Hold Short Operations (LAHSO)

Completion Standards

The lesson will have been successfully completed when the student answers the questions in Study Unit 3, "Airports, Air Traffic Control, and Airspace," of *Private Pilot FAA Knowledge Test Prep*, FAA Test Prep Online, and/or Online Ground School with a minimum passing grade of 80%.

	Dates Studied	Date Completed
Pilot Handbook	____ ____ ____ ____ ____	____
Private Pilot FAA Knowledge Test Prep	____ ____ ____ ____ ____	____

Notes:

GROUND LESSON 4: FEDERAL AVIATION REGULATIONS

Objective

To develop the student's knowledge of pertinent Federal Aviation Regulations (14 CFR) and the accident-reporting rules of the National Transportation Safety Board (NTSB).

Text References

Pilot Handbook, Study Unit 4, "Federal Aviation Regulations"
Private Pilot FAA Knowledge Test Prep, Study Unit 4, "Federal Aviation Regulations" (except Subunit 4.7, "Recreational Pilot Related Federal Aviation Regulations")

Pilot Handbook Study Unit 4 Contents	*Private Pilot FAA Knowledge Test Prep* Study Unit 4 Contents
4.1 Federal Aviation Regulations 4.2 Part 1 -- Definitions and Abbreviations 4.3 Part 21 -- Certification Procedures for Products and Articles 4.4 Part 39 -- Airworthiness Directives 4.5 Part 43 -- Maintenance, Preventive Maintenance, Rebuilding, and Alteration 4.6 Part 61 -- Certification: Pilots, Flight Instructors, and Ground Instructors 4.7 Part 67 -- Medical Standards and Certification 4.8 Part 91 -- General Operating and Flight Rules 4.9 NTSB Part 830 -- Notification and Reporting of Aircraft Accidents or Incidents and Overdue Aircraft, and Preservation of Aircraft Wreckage, Mail, Cargo, and Records 4.10 Summary of Current 14 CFR Part Numbers	4.1 14 CFR Part 1 4.2 14 CFR Part 21 4.3 14 CFR Part 39 4.4 14 CFR Part 43 4.5 14 CFR Part 47 4.6 14 CFR Part 61 4.8 14 CFR Part 91: 91.3 – 91.151 4.9 14 CFR Part 91: 91.159 – 91.519 4.10 NTSB Part 830

Completion Standards

The lesson will have been successfully completed when the student answers the questions in Study Unit 4, "Federal Aviation Regulations," of *Private Pilot FAA Knowledge Test Prep*, FAA Test Prep Online, and/or Online Ground School with a minimum passing grade of 80%.

	Dates Studied	Date Completed
Pilot Handbook	___ ___ ___ ___ ___	___
Private Pilot FAA Knowledge Test Prep	___ ___ ___ ___ ___	___

Notes:

GROUND LESSON 5: AIRPLANE PERFORMANCE AND WEIGHT AND BALANCE

Objective

To develop the student's ability to determine airplane performance, including weight and balance. Additionally, the student will learn the adverse effects of exceeding the airplane's limitations.

Text References

Pilot Handbook, Study Unit 5, "Airplane Performance and Weight and Balance"
Private Pilot FAA Knowledge Test Prep, Study Unit 5, "Airplane Performance and Weight and Balance"

Pilot Handbook Study Unit 5 Contents	*Private Pilot FAA Knowledge Test Prep* Study Unit 5 Contents
5.1 Determinants of Airplane Performance	5.1 Density Altitude
5.2 Standard Atmosphere	5.2 Density Altitude Computations
5.3 Pressure Altitude	5.3 Takeoff Distance
5.4 Density Altitude	5.4 Cruise Power Settings
5.5 Takeoff Performance	5.5 Crosswind Components
5.6 Climb Performance	5.6 Landing Distance
5.7 Cruise and Range Performance	5.7 Weight and Balance Definitions
5.8 Glide Performance	5.8 Center of Gravity Calculations
5.9 Crosswind Performance	5.9 Center of Gravity Graphs
5.10 Landing Performance	5.10 Center of Gravity Tables
5.11 Stall Speed Performance	
5.12 Weight and Balance Overview	
5.13 Weight and Balance Management	
5.14 Weight and Balance Terms	
5.15 Basic Principles of Weight and Balance	
5.16 Methods of Determining Weight and Balance	
5.17 Center of Gravity Calculations	
5.18 Center of Gravity Charts	
5.19 Center of Gravity Tables	
5.20 Weight Change and Weight Shift Computations	

Completion Standards

The lesson will have been successfully completed when the student answers the questions in Study Unit 5, "Airplane Performance and Weight and Balance," of *Private Pilot FAA Knowledge Test Prep*, FAA Test Prep Online, and/or Online Ground School with a minimum passing grade of 80%.

	Dates Studied	Date Completed
Pilot Handbook	____ ____ ____ ____ ____	____
Private Pilot FAA Knowledge Test Prep	____ ____ ____ ____ ____	____

Notes:

STAGE ONE KNOWLEDGE TEST

Objective

To evaluate the student's understanding of the material presented during Ground Lesson 1 through Ground Lesson 5. The Stage One knowledge test consists of 25 questions on pages 67-69.

Content

<u>Lesson</u>
1   Airplanes and Aerodynamics
2   Airplane Instruments, Engines, and Systems
3   Airports, Air Traffic Control, and Airspace
4   Federal Aviation Regulations
5   Airplane Performance and Weight and Balance

Completion Standards

The lesson will have been successfully completed when the student has completed the Stage One knowledge test with a minimum passing grade of 80%.

STAGE TWO

Stage Two Objective

To develop the student's knowledge of medical factors and the aeronautical decision-making process related to all flights. The student will learn how weather affects flying. The student will learn how to obtain weather briefings and how to interpret aviation reports, forecasts, and charts. Additionally, the student will learn how to use navigation charts, plotters, flight computers, and flight publications for cross-country flight planning. Finally, the student will learn how to use various navigation systems.

Stage Two Completion Standards

Stage Two will have been successfully completed when the student passes the Stage Two knowledge test with a minimum passing grade of 80%.

Lesson	Topic	Min. Time
6	Aeromedical Factors and Aeronautical Decision Making (ADM)	2.0
7	Aviation Weather	3.0
8	Aviation Weather Services	2.5
9	Navigation: Charts and Publications	3.0
10	Navigation Systems	2.5
11	Cross-Country Flight Planning	2.5
	Stage Two Knowledge Test	1.0
	End-of-Course Knowledge Test	2.5

GROUND LESSON 6: AEROMEDICAL FACTORS AND AERONAUTICAL DECISION MAKING (ADM)

Objective

To develop the student's knowledge of the medical factors related to flight and to the aeronautical decision making (ADM) process.

Text References

Pilot Handbook, Study Unit 6, "Aeromedical Factors and Aeronautical Decision Making (ADM)"
Private Pilot FAA Knowledge Test Prep, Study Unit 6, "Aeromedical Factors and Aeronautical Decision Making (ADM)"

Pilot Handbook Study Unit 6 Contents	*Private Pilot FAA Knowledge Test Prep* Study Unit 6 Contents
6.1 Fitness for Flight 6.2 Hypoxia 6.3 Dehydration 6.4 Hyperventilation 6.5 Carbon Monoxide Poisoning 6.6 Decompression Sickness after Scuba Diving 6.7 Motion Sickness 6.8 Sinus and Ear Block 6.9 Spatial Disorientation 6.10 Illusions in Flight 6.11 Vision 6.12 Aeronautical Decision Making (ADM) 6.13 Weather-Related Decision Making 6.14 Stress and Flying 6.15 Identifying the Enemy 6.16 Single-Pilot Resource Management (SRM) 6.17 Automation Management	6.1 Hypoxia 6.2 Hyperventilation 6.3 Spatial Disorientation 6.4 Vision 6.5 Carbon Monoxide 6.6 Aeronautical Decision Making (ADM) and Judgment

Completion Standards

The lesson will have been successfully completed when the student answers the questions in Study Unit 6, "Aeromedical Factors and Aeronautical Decision Making (ADM)," of *Private Pilot FAA Knowledge Test Prep*, FAA Test Prep Online, and/or Online Ground School with a minimum passing grade of 80%.

	Dates Studied	Date Completed
Pilot Handbook	___ ___ ___ ___ ___	___
Private Pilot FAA Knowledge Test Prep	___ ___ ___ ___ ___	___

Notes:

GROUND LESSON 7: AVIATION WEATHER

Objective

To develop the student's knowledge of the fundamentals of weather, as associated with the operation of an airplane.

Text References

Pilot Handbook, Study Unit 7, "Aviation Weather"
Private Pilot FAA Knowledge Test Prep, Study Unit 7, "Aviation Weather"

Pilot Handbook Study Unit 7 Contents	*Private Pilot FAA Knowledge Test Prep* Study Unit 7 Contents
7.1 The Earth's Atmosphere 7.2 Temperature 7.3 Atmospheric Pressure 7.4 Wind 7.5 Moisture, Cloud Formation, and Precipitation 7.6 Stable and Unstable Air 7.7 Clouds 7.8 Air Masses and Fronts 7.9 Turbulence 7.10 Icing 7.11 Thunderstorms 7.12 Fog	7.1 Causes of Weather 7.2 Convective Currents 7.3 Fronts 7.4 Thunderstorms 7.5 Icing 7.6 Mountain Wave 7.7 Wind Shear Avoidance 7.8 Temperature/Dew Point and Fog 7.9 Clouds 7.10 Stability of Air Masses 7.11 Temperature Inversions

Completion Standards

The lesson will have been successfully completed when the student answers the questions in Study Unit 7, "Aviation Weather," of *Private Pilot FAA Knowledge Test Prep*, FAA Test Prep Online, and/or Online Ground School with a minimum passing grade of 80%.

	Dates Studied	Date Completed
Pilot Handbook	___ ___ ___ ___ ___	___
Private Pilot FAA Knowledge Test Prep	___ ___ ___ ___ ___	___

Notes:

GROUND LESSON 8: AVIATION WEATHER SERVICES

Objective

To develop the student's ability to interpret and use weather charts, reports, forecasts, and broadcasts and to develop the student's knowledge of the procedure to obtain weather briefings.

Text References

Pilot Handbook, Study Unit 8, "Aviation Weather Services"
Private Pilot FAA Knowledge Test Prep, Study Unit 8, "Aviation Weather Services"

Pilot Handbook Study Unit 8 Contents	*Private Pilot FAA Knowledge Test Prep* Study Unit 8 Contents
8.1 Flight Service Station (FSS) 8.2 Aviation Routine Weather Report (METAR) 8.3 Pilot Weather Report (PIREP) 8.4 Terminal Aerodrome Forecast (TAF) 8.5 Graphical Airman's Meteorological Advisory (G-AIRMET) 8.6 Graphical Forecasts for Aviation (GFA) 8.7 In-Flight Aviation Weather Advisories 8.8 Winds and Temperatures Aloft Forecast (FB) 8.9 Surface Analysis Chart 8.10 Ceiling and Visibility Analysis (CVA) 8.11 Radar Observations 8.12 Short-Range Surface Prognostic (PROG) Chart 8.13 Low-Level Significant Weather (SIGWX) Chart 8.14 Leidos Flight Service Online 8.15 Aviation Weather Resources on the Internet	8.1 Weather Briefings 8.2 Aviation Routine Weather Report (METAR) 8.3 Pilot Weather Report (PIREP) 8.4 Terminal Aerodrome Forecast (TAF) 8.5 Radar Weather Reports 8.6 In-Flight Weather 8.7 Wind and Temperature Aloft Forecasts (FB) 8.8 Significant Weather Prognostic Charts 8.9 AIRMETs and SIGMETs

Completion Standards

The lesson will have been successfully completed when the student answers the questions in Study Unit 8, "Aviation Weather Services," of *Private Pilot FAA Knowledge Test Prep*, FAA Test Prep Online, and/or Online Ground School with a minimum passing grade of 80%.

	Dates Studied	Date Completed
Pilot Handbook	____ ____ ____ ____ ____	____
Private Pilot FAA Knowledge Test Prep	____ ____ ____ ____ ____	____

Notes:

GROUND LESSON 9: NAVIGATION: CHARTS AND PUBLICATIONS

Objective

To develop the student's knowledge of, and the ability to use, navigation charts, publications, and a flight computer in planning a VFR cross-country flight.

Text References

Pilot Handbook, Study Unit 9, "Navigation: Charts, Publications, Flight Computers"
Private Pilot FAA Knowledge Test Prep, Study Unit 9, "Navigation: Charts and Publications"

Pilot Handbook Study Unit 9 Contents	*Private Pilot FAA Knowledge Test Prep* Study Unit 9 Contents
9.1 VFR Navigation Charts	9.1 Longitude and Latitude
9.2 Longitude and Latitude	9.2 Airspace and Altitudes
9.3 Sectional Chart Symbology	9.3 Identifying Landmarks
9.4 FAA Advisory Circulars (ACs)	9.4 Radio Frequencies
9.5 *Aeronautical Information Manual (AIM)*	9.5 FAA Advisory Circulars
9.6 Chart Supplement U.S.	9.6 Chart Supplements
9.7 Notice to Airmen (NOTAM) System	9.7 Notices to Airmen (NOTAMs)
9.8 Flight Computers	
9.9 The Gleim Flight Computer	
9.10 The Calculator Side of the Flight Computer	
9.11 Conversion of Nautical Miles to Statute Miles and Vice Versa	
9.12 Speed, Distance, and Time Computations	
9.13 Fuel Computations	
9.14 True Airspeed and Density Altitude	
9.15 Corrected (Approximately True) Altitude	
9.16 Off-Course Correction	
9.17 Radius of Action	
9.18 Other Conversions	
9.19 Temperature Conversions	
9.20 The Wind Side of the Gleim Flight Computer	
9.21 Determining Magnetic Heading and Groundspeed	
9.22 Determining Wind Direction and Speed	
9.23 Determining Altitude for Most Favorable Winds	
9.24 Alternative: E6B Computer Approach to Magnetic Heading	
9.25 Information Side of Sliding Card (Gleim E6B)	
9.26 Electronic Flight Computers	

Completion Standards

The lesson will have been successfully completed when the student answers the questions in Study Unit 9, "Navigation: Charts and Publications," of *Private Pilot FAA Knowledge Test Prep*, FAA Test Prep Online, and/or Online Ground School with a minimum passing grade of 80%.

	Dates Studied	Date Completed
Pilot Handbook	____ ____ ____ ____ ____	____
Private Pilot FAA Knowledge Test Prep	____ ____ ____ ____ ____	____

Notes:

GROUND LESSON 10: NAVIGATION SYSTEMS

Objective

To develop the student's knowledge of various navigation systems.

Text References

Pilot Handbook, Study Unit 10, "Navigation Systems"
Private Pilot FAA Knowledge Test Prep, Study Unit 10, "Navigation Systems"

Pilot Handbook Study Unit 10 Contents	*Private Pilot FAA Knowledge Test Prep* Study Unit 10 Contents
10.1 Characteristics of Radio Waves 10.2 VHF Omnidirectional Range (VOR) 10.3 Distance-Measuring Equipment (DME) 10.4 Automatic Direction Finder (ADF) 10.5 Radio Magnetic Indicator (RMI) 10.6 Area Navigation (RNAV) 10.7 VORTAC-Based RNAV 10.8 Global Positioning System (GPS)	10.1 VOR Test Facility (VOT) 10.2 Determining Position Using VORs 10.3 Global Positioning System (GPS) 10.4 Pilotage and Dead Reckoning

Completion Standards

The lesson will have been successfully completed when the student answers the questions in Study Unit 10, "Navigation Systems," of *Private Pilot FAA Knowledge Test Prep*, FAA Test Prep Online, and/or Online Ground School with a minimum passing grade of 80%.

	Dates Studied	Date Completed
Pilot Handbook	____ ____ ____ ____ ____	____
Private Pilot FAA Knowledge Test Prep	____ ____ ____ ____ ____	____

Notes:

GROUND LESSON 11: CROSS-COUNTRY FLIGHT PLANNING

Objective

To further develop the student's ability to properly plan a VFR cross-country flight. Additionally, the student is introduced to the procedures to use when lost and when diverting to an alternate airport.

Text References

Pilot Handbook, Study Unit 11, "Cross-Country Flight Planning" (except Subunit 7, "IFR Cross-Country Procedures")
Private Pilot FAA Knowledge Test Prep, Study Unit 11, "Cross-Country Flight Planning"

Pilot Handbook Study Unit 11 Contents	*Private Pilot FAA Knowledge Test Prep* Study Unit 11 Contents
11.1 Preflight Preparation 11.2 Flight Plan (ICAO) 11.3 Weight and Balance 11.4 Navigation 11.5 Diversion to an Alternate Airport 11.6 Lost Procedures	11.1 VFR Flight Plan 11.2 Preflight Inspection 11.3 Miscellaneous Airspeed Questions 11.4 Taxiing Technique 11.5 Magnetic Course 11.6 Magnetic Heading 11.7 Compass Heading 11.8 Time En Route 11.9 Time Zone Corrections 11.10 Fundamentals of Flight 11.11 Rectangular Course 11.12 S-Turns across a Road 11.13 Landings

Completion Standards

The lesson will have been successfully completed when the student answers the questions in Study Unit 11, "Cross-Country Flight Planning," of *Private Pilot FAA Knowledge Test Prep*, FAA Test Prep Online, and/or Online Ground School with a minimum passing grade of 80%.

	Dates Studied	Date Completed
Pilot Handbook	____ ____ ____ ____ ____	____
Private Pilot FAA Knowledge Test Prep	____ ____ ____ ____ ____	____

Notes:

STAGE TWO KNOWLEDGE TEST

Objective

To evaluate the student's understanding of the material presented during Ground Lesson 6 through Ground Lesson 11. The Stage Two knowledge test consists of 25 questions on pages 70-71.

Content

<u>Lesson</u>
6   Aeromedical Factors and Aeronautical Decision Making (ADM)
7   Aviation Weather
8   Aviation Weather Services
9   Navigation: Charts and Publications
10   Navigation Systems
11   Cross-Country Flight Planning

Completion Standards

The lesson will have been successfully completed when the student has completed the Stage Two knowledge test with a minimum passing grade of 80%.

END-OF-COURSE KNOWLEDGE TEST

Objective

To evaluate the student's comprehension of the material covered in the ground training course (lessons 1-11) and to determine the student's readiness to take the FAA private pilot knowledge test. The end-of-course knowledge test consists of 60 questions on pages 72-76.

Content

Practice Private Pilot Knowledge Test

Completion Standards

The lesson will have been successfully completed when the student has completed the practice private pilot knowledge test with a minimum passing grade of 80%.

PRIVATE PILOT
FLIGHT TRAINING SYLLABUS
AIRPLANE SINGLE-ENGINE LAND

FLIGHT TRAINING COURSE OBJECTIVES

The student will obtain the aeronautical knowledge and experience and demonstrate the flight proficiency necessary to meet the requirements for a private pilot certificate with an airplane category rating and single-engine land class rating.

FLIGHT TRAINING COURSE COMPLETION STANDARDS

The student will demonstrate through the stage checks and school records that (s)he has the necessary flight proficiency and aeronautical experience to obtain a private pilot certificate with an airplane category rating and single-engine land class rating.

Lesson	Topic
	Stage One
1	Introduction to Flight
2	Four Fundamentals of Flight
3	Basic Instrument Maneuvers
4	Slow Flight and Stalls
5	Emergency Operations
6	Performance Maneuvers
7	Review
8	Go-Around and Forward Slip to a Landing
9	Presolo Review
10	Presolo Review
11	First Solo
12	Stage One Check
	Stage Two
13	Second Solo
14	Short-Field and Soft-Field Takeoffs and Landings
15	Solo Maneuvers Review
16	Navigation Systems
17	Dual Cross-Country
18	Night Flight -- Local
19	Night Cross-Country
20	Solo Cross-Country (Part 61/141)
20A	Solo Cross-Country (Part 61)
20B	Solo Cross-Country or Local Flight (Part 61)
21	Maneuvers Review
22	Solo Practice
23	Maneuvers Review
24	Solo Practice
25	Stage Two Check
26	End of Course Test

The following is a brief description of the parts of each flight lesson in this syllabus:

Objective: We open each lesson with an objective, usually a sentence or two, to help you gain perspective and understand the goal for that particular lesson.

Text References: For lessons with new learning items, this section tells you which reference books you will need to study or refer to while mastering the tasks within the lesson. Abbreviations are given to facilitate the cross-referencing process.

Content: Each lesson contains a list of the tasks required to be completed before moving to the next lesson. A task may be listed as a "review item" (a task that was covered in a previous lesson) or as a "new item" (a task which is introduced to you for the first time). Each task is preceded by three blank "checkoff" boxes, which may be used by your CFI to keep track of your progress and to indicate that each task was completed.

There are three boxes because it may take more than one flight to complete the lesson. Your CFI may mark the box(es) next to each task in one of the following methods (or any other method desired):

✓ - task completed to lesson completion standards	D - demonstrated by instructor A - accomplished by you S - safe/satisfactory C - meets or exceeds ACS standards	1 - above lesson standard 2 - meets lesson standard 3 - below lesson standard

The last task in each flight lesson is labeled "Additional items at CFI's discretion," and is followed by several blank lines. This area can be used to record any extra items that your CFI feels are appropriate to the lesson, taking into account such variables as weather, local operational considerations, and your progress as a student.

NOTE: CFIs are reminded not to limit themselves to the blank lines provided–use as much of the page as you need.

Completion Standards: Based on these standards, your CFI determines how well you have met the objective of the lesson in terms of knowledge and skill.

Instructor's Comments and Lesson Assignment: Space is provided for your CFI's critique of the lesson, which you can refer to later. Your instructor may also write any specific assignment for the next lesson.

Reading Assignments for Flight Lessons

You are expected to be prepared for each flight lesson. Our reading assignments include text references for new tasks to help you understand what is going to happen and how and why you need to do everything **before** you go to the airport.

Next to each new item in the **Content** section, we provide study unit-level references to read in *Private Pilot Flight Maneuvers and Practical Test Prep* (FM) and/or *Pilot Handbook* (PH) and the section to read, if appropriate, in your airplane's Pilot's Operating Handbook (POH). You can make use of the comprehensive index in the Gleim books if you need to analyze specific task element-level details.

Study Tips

- As you read the material, attempt to understand the basic concepts.
- Try to anticipate and visualize the concepts and flight maneuvers.
- With this basic knowledge, your CFI can expand on the specific and finer points, especially when explaining how a task is done in your specific airplane.
- After your flight lesson, task items are fresh in your mind; they will make sense, and you should be able to understand and learn more.
- Study review items so you can explain them to your CFI and your examiner.
- After you study, relax and plan a time to begin preparing for the next flight lesson.

STAGE ONE

Stage One Objective

The student will obtain the basic flying procedures and skills necessary for the first solo flight.

Stage One Completion Standards

The stage will be completed when the student satisfactorily passes the Stage One check and is able to conduct solo flights safely.

Lesson	Topic
	Stage One
1	Introduction to Flight
2	Four Fundamentals of Flight
3	Basic Instrument Maneuvers
4	Slow Flight and Stalls
5	Emergency Operations
6	Performance Maneuvers
7	Review
8	Go-Around and Forward Slip to a Landing
9	Presolo Review
10	Presolo Review
11	First Solo
12	Stage One Check

FLIGHT LESSON 1: INTRODUCTION TO FLIGHT

Objective

To familiarize the student with the training airplane, its operating characteristics, cockpit controls, and the instruments and systems. The student will be introduced to preflight and postflight procedures, the use of checklists, and the safety precautions to be followed. Additionally, the student will be introduced to the effect and use of the flight controls and the local practice area and airport.

Text References

Private Pilot Flight Maneuvers and Practical Test Prep (FM)
Pilot Handbook (PH)
Pilot's Operating Handbook (POH)

Content

1. Preflight briefing
2. New items
   - ☐☐☐ Preflight preparation - CFI
     - ☐☐☐ Pilot qualifications - FM 3
     - ☐☐☐ Airplane logbooks - CFI
     - ☐☐☐ Airworthiness requirements - FM 4
   - ☐☐☐ Preflight procedures - CFI
     - ☐☐☐ Use of checklists - FM 12; POH 4
     - ☐☐☐ Preflight assessment - FM 11; POH 4
     - ☐☐☐ Airplane servicing - CFI
   - ☐☐☐ Location of emergency equipment and survival gear - CFI
   - ☐☐☐ Operation of airplane systems - POH 7; CFI
   - ☐☐☐ Engine starting - FM 13; POH 4
   - ☐☐☐ Taxiing - FM 14; POH 4
   - ☐☐☐ Runway incursion avoidance - FM 14; PH 3
   - ☐☐☐ Before takeoff check - FM 15; POH 4
   - ☐☐☐ Normal and crosswind takeoff and climb - FM 18; POH 4
   - ☐☐☐ Effect and use of primary flight controls and trim - PH 1
   - ☐☐☐ Practice area familiarization - CFI
   - ☐☐☐ Collision and obstacle avoidance and scanning - FM 17
   - ☐☐☐ Normal and crosswind approach and landing - FM 19; POH 4
   - ☐☐☐ After landing procedures - FM 47; POH 4
   - ☐☐☐ Parking and securing the airplane - FM 47; POH 4
   - ☐☐☐ Additional items at CFI's discretion _____
   _____
   _____
3. Postflight critique and preview of next lesson

Completion Standards

The lesson will have been successfully completed when the student displays an understanding of the airplane's systems, the use of checklists, preflight procedures, and postflight procedures. Additionally, the student will be familiar with the correct use of the controls, the local practice area, and the airport.

Instructor's comments:_____

_____

Lesson assignment:_____

_____

Notes:_____

_____

_____

_____

FLIGHT LESSON 2: FOUR FUNDAMENTALS OF FLIGHT

Objective

To develop the student's skill in the performance of the four basic flight maneuvers (straight-and-level, turns, climbs, and descents). Additionally, the student will be introduced to radio communication procedures, airport markings, and traffic patterns.

Text References

Private Pilot Flight Maneuvers and Practical Test Prep (FM)
Pilot Handbook (PH)
Pilot's Operating Handbook (POH)

Content

1. Flight Lesson 1 complete? Yes ___   Copy of lesson placed in student's folder? Yes ___
2. Preflight briefing
3. Review items

☐☐☐ Use of checklists
☐☐☐ Pilot qualifications
☐☐☐ Preflight assessment
☐☐☐ Engine starting
☐☐☐ Taxiing
☐☐☐ Runway incursion avoidance
☐☐☐ Before takeoff check

☐☐☐ Normal and crosswind takeoff and climb
☐☐☐ Collision and obstacle avoidance and scanning
☐☐☐ Normal and crosswind approach and landing
☐☐☐ After landing, parking, and securing procedures

4. New items

☐☐☐ Flight deck management - FM 12
☐☐☐ Radio communication - FM 16; PH 3
☐☐☐ Airport markings and signs - PH 3
☐☐☐ Traffic patterns - FM 17; PH 3
☐☐☐ Straight-and-level flight - FM App C
☐☐☐ Climbs and climbing turns - FM App C; POH 4
  ☐☐☐ Cruise climb
  ☐☐☐ Best rate of climb
  ☐☐☐ Best angle of climb
☐☐☐ Turns to headings - FM 39, App C

☐☐☐ Descents and descending turns - FM App C; POH 4
  ☐☐☐ Cruise descent
  ☐☐☐ Traffic pattern descent
  ☐☐☐ Power-off glide
☐☐☐ Level-off from climbs and descents - FM App C
☐☐☐ Torque effects - PH 1
☐☐☐ Additional items at CFI's discretion _____

5. Postflight critique and preview of next lesson

Completion Standards

The lesson will have been successfully completed when the student can, with instructor assistance, conduct a preflight inspection, properly use checklists, taxi, perform a before-takeoff check, and make a normal and crosswind takeoff. Additionally, the student will display an understanding of the four fundamentals of flight and the various climb and descent attitudes.

Instructor's comments:_____

_____

Lesson assignment:_____

_____

Notes:_____

_____

_____

FLIGHT LESSON 3: BASIC INSTRUMENT MANEUVERS

Objective

To improve the student's proficiency in the four fundamentals of flight and to introduce the student to basic instrument maneuvers.

Text References

Private Pilot Flight Maneuvers and Practical Test Prep (FM)

Content

1. Flight Lesson 2 complete? Yes ___   Copy of lesson placed in student's folder? Yes ___
2. Preflight briefing
3. Review items

□□□ Use of checklists
□□□ Radio communication
□□□ Pilot qualifications
□□□ Preflight assessment
□□□ Engine starting
□□□ Taxiing
□□□ Runway incursion avoidance
□□□ Before takeoff check
□□□ Normal and crosswind takeoff and climb

□□□ Straight-and-level flight
□□□ Climbs
□□□ Descents
□□□ Turns to a heading
□□□ Collision and obstacle avoidance and scanning
□□□ Traffic patterns
□□□ Normal and crosswind approach
□□□ After landing, parking, and securing procedures

4. New items

□□□ Taxiing in a crosswind - FM 14
□□□ Attitude instrument flying - FM 36
□□□ Straight-and-level flight (IR)* - FM 36
□□□ Constant airspeed climbs (IR)* - FM 37
□□□ Constant airspeed descents (IR)* - FM 38

□□□ Turns to headings (IR)* - FM 39
□□□ Additional items at CFI's discretion _____

* IR means instrument references only, which can be taught by CFIs in contrast to IFR training by CFIIs.

5. Postflight critique and preview of next lesson

Completion Standards

The lesson will have been successfully completed when the student demonstrates an increased understanding of the four fundamentals of flight by use of proper controls. The student will, with instructor assistance, become more proficient in the preflight procedures and a normal and crosswind takeoff. Additionally, the student will display an understanding of the basic instrument maneuvers.

Instructor's comments: _____

_____

Lesson assignment: _____

_____

Notes: _____

_____

_____

_____

_____

FLIGHT LESSON 4: SLOW FLIGHT AND STALLS

Objective

To improve the student's proficiency in the performance of the four fundamentals of flight and to introduce maneuvering during slow flight, stalls, and spin awareness.

Text References

Private Pilot Flight Maneuvers and Practical Test Prep (FM)
Pilot Handbook (PH)
Pilot's Operating Handbook (POH)

Content

1. Flight Lesson 3 complete? Yes ⎯⎯   Copy of lesson placed in student's folder? Yes ⎯⎯
2. Preflight briefing
3. Review items

☐☐☐ Use of checklists
☐☐☐ Operation of airplane systems
☐☐☐ Preflight assessment
☐☐☐ Collision and obstacle avoidance and scanning
☐☐☐ Engine starting
☐☐☐ Radio communication
☐☐☐ Airport markings and signs
☐☐☐ Taxiing

☐☐☐ Runway incursion avoidance
☐☐☐ Before takeoff check
☐☐☐ Normal and crosswind takeoff and climb
☐☐☐ Four fundamentals of flight
☐☐☐ Traffic patterns
☐☐☐ Normal and crosswind approach and landing
☐☐☐ After landing, parking, and securing procedures

4. New items

☐☐☐ Maneuvering during slow flight - FM 32; PH 1
☐☐☐ Stall awareness - FM 33, FM 34
☐☐☐ Power-off stalls (entered from straight flight) - FM 33; PH 1
☐☐☐ Power-on stalls (entered from straight flight) - FM 34; PH 1
☐☐☐ Spin awareness - FM 35; PH 1; POH 3
☐☐☐ Additional items at CFI's discretion ⎯⎯⎯⎯⎯⎯⎯⎯⎯⎯⎯⎯⎯⎯⎯⎯⎯⎯⎯⎯⎯⎯

5. Postflight critique and preview of next lesson

Completion Standards

The lesson will have been successfully completed when the student displays proficiency in the four fundamentals of flight by maintaining altitude, ±250 ft.; airspeed, ±20 kt.; and heading, ±20°. During this and subsequent flight lessons, the student will be proficient in the preflight inspection, engine starting, taxiing, the before-takeoff check, and the postflight procedures without instructor assistance. The student will perform normal and crosswind takeoffs without instructor assistance. The student will show an increase in proficiency in traffic patterns and approaches with the instructor still performing the landing. Finally, the student will display an understanding of maneuvering during slow flight, the indications of an approaching stall, the proper recovery procedures, and the conditions necessary for a spin to occur.

Instructor's comments:⎯⎯⎯⎯⎯⎯⎯⎯⎯⎯⎯⎯⎯⎯⎯⎯⎯⎯⎯⎯⎯⎯⎯⎯⎯⎯⎯⎯⎯⎯⎯⎯⎯⎯⎯

⎯⎯

Lesson assignment:⎯⎯⎯⎯⎯⎯⎯⎯⎯⎯⎯⎯⎯⎯⎯⎯⎯⎯⎯⎯⎯⎯⎯⎯⎯⎯⎯⎯⎯⎯⎯⎯⎯⎯⎯⎯⎯⎯

⎯⎯

Notes:⎯⎯⎯

⎯⎯

FLIGHT LESSON 5: EMERGENCY OPERATIONS

Objective

To improve the student's proficiency while maneuvering during slow flight and the recognition of and correct recovery from stalls. Additionally, the student will be introduced to emergency operations and normal landings.

Text References

Private Pilot Flight Maneuvers and Practical Test Prep (FM)
Pilot's Operating Handbook (POH)

Content

1. Flight Lesson 4 complete? Yes ___   Copy of lesson placed in student's folder? Yes ___
2. Preflight briefing
3. Review items
   - ☐☐☐ Maneuvering during slow flight
   - ☐☐☐ Power-off stalls (entered from straight flight)
   - ☐☐☐ Power-on stalls (entered from straight flight)
   - ☐☐☐ Spin awareness
   - ☐☐☐ Normal and crosswind takeoff and approach

4. New items
   - ☐☐☐ Emergency descent - FM 42; POH 3
   - ☐☐☐ Emergency approach and landing - FM 43; POH 3
   - ☐☐☐ Systems and equipment malfunctions - FM 44; POH 3
   - ☐☐☐ Emergency equipment and survival gear - FM 45
   - ☐☐☐ Emergencies during takeoff roll, initial climb, cruise, descent, and in the traffic pattern - FM 42-44; POH 3
   - ☐☐☐ Normal and crosswind landing - FM 19
   - ☐☐☐ Recovery from bouncing and ballooning during landing - FM 19
   - ☐☐☐ Additional items at CFI's discretion _____

5. Postflight critique and preview of next lesson

Completion Standards

The lesson will have been successfully completed when the student displays an understanding of the procedures to be used during various emergency operations and will be able to make a normal landing with instructor assistance. Additionally, the student will demonstrate improved proficiency in maneuvering during slow flight and improved recognition of and recovery from stalls. The student will be able to maintain altitude, ±200 ft.; airspeed, ±15 kt.; and heading, ±20° during straight-and-level flight.

Instructor's comments: _____

_____

Lesson assignment: _____

_____

Notes: _____

_____

_____

_____

FLIGHT LESSON 6: PERFORMANCE MANEUVERS

Objective

To review previous lessons to gain proficiency and to introduce the student to steep turns and ground reference maneuvers.

Text References

Private Pilot Flight Maneuvers and Practical Test Prep (FM)
Pilot Handbook (PH)

Content

1. Flight Lesson 5 complete? Yes ___   Copy of lesson placed in student's folder? Yes ___
2. Preflight briefing
3. Review items
   - ☐☐☐ Normal and crosswind takeoff and landing
   - ☐☐☐ Emergency descent
   - ☐☐☐ Systems and equipment malfunctions
   - ☐☐☐ Emergency approach and landing

4. New items
   - ☐☐☐ Steep turns - FM 26
   - ☐☐☐ Rectangular course - FM 27
   - ☐☐☐ S-turns - FM 27
   - ☐☐☐ Turns around a point - FM 27
   - ☐☐☐ Wake turbulence avoidance - PH 3
   - ☐☐☐ Additional items at CFI's discretion _____

5. Postflight critique and preview of next lesson

Completion Standards

The lesson will have been successfully completed when the student demonstrates the proper entry procedures and understands how to maintain a specific ground track during the performance of ground reference maneuvers. Additionally, the student will demonstrate increased proficiency in emergency procedures. The student will be able to maintain altitude, ±200 ft.; airspeed, ±15 kt.; and heading, ±20°.

Instructor's comments:_____

Lesson assignment:_____

Notes:_____

FLIGHT LESSON 7: REVIEW

Objective

To review previous lessons to gain proficiency in the flight maneuvers. Additionally, stalls should be entered from straight flight and turns.

Content

1. Flight Lesson 6 complete? Yes ___   Copy of lesson placed in student's folder? Yes ___
2. Preflight briefing
3. Review items
   - ☐☐☐ Normal and crosswind takeoff and landing
   - ☐☐☐ Maneuvering during slow flight
   - ☐☐☐ Power-off stalls (entered from straight flight and turns)
   - ☐☐☐ Power-on stalls (entered from straight flight and turns)
   - ☐☐☐ Steep turns
   - ☐☐☐ Emergency approach and landing
   - ☐☐☐ Turns around a point
   - ☐☐☐ S-turns
   - ☐☐☐ Rectangular course
   - ☐☐☐ Recovery from faulty approaches and landings
   - ☐☐☐ Additional items at CFI's discretion _____

4. Postflight critique and preview of next lesson

Completion Standards

The lesson will have been successfully completed when the student demonstrates increased proficiency while performing the maneuvers. During the ground reference maneuvers, the student will maintain altitude, ±200 ft.; and airspeed, ±15 kt.

Instructor's comments: _____

Lesson assignment: _____

Notes: _____

FLIGHT LESSON 8: GO-AROUND AND FORWARD SLIP TO A LANDING

Objective

To introduce the student to go-around procedures, forward slip to a landing, and recovery from bouncing and ballooning during landing. Additionally, the student will gain proficiency in takeoffs and landings through concentrated practice.

Text References

Private Pilot Flight Maneuvers and Practical Test Prep (FM)

Content

1. Flight Lesson 7 complete? Yes ___   Copy of lesson placed in student's folder? Yes ___
2. Preflight briefing
3. Review items

    ☐☐☐ Normal and crosswind takeoffs and landings
    ☐☐☐ Traffic patterns
    ☐☐☐ Recovery from bouncing and ballooning during landing
    _____

4. New items

    ☐☐☐ Go-around/rejected landing - FM 25
    ☐☐☐ Forward slip to a landing - FM 24
    ☐☐☐ Dealing with unexpected requests from ATC - CFI
        ☐☐☐ Cross airport to opposite downwind - CFI
        ☐☐☐ Reverse direction on downwind - CFI
        ☐☐☐ Teardrop maneuver back to final approach from the upwind leg due to a runway change - CFI
    ☐☐☐ ATC light signals - FM 16
    ☐☐☐ Wind shear avoidance - FM 17
    ☐☐☐ Additional items at CFI's discretion _____
    _____

5. Postflight critique and preview of next lesson

Completion Standards

The lesson will have been successfully completed when the student can demonstrate an understanding of the go-around procedures, forward slip to a landing, and the recovery from bouncing and ballooning during a landing. Additionally, the student will demonstrate the ability to fly a specific ground track during the performance of ground reference maneuvers. In the traffic pattern, the student will be able to maintain altitude, ±200 ft.; airspeed, ±15 kt.; and desired heading, ±20°.

Instructor's comments: _____

_____

Lesson assignment: _____

_____

Notes: _____

_____

_____

_____

_____

_____

FLIGHT LESSON 9: PRESOLO REVIEW

Objective

To review and to further develop the student's proficiency in the maneuvers and procedures required for solo flight.

Content

1. Flight Lesson 8 complete? Yes ___   Copy of lesson placed in student's folder? Yes ___
2. Preflight briefing
3. Review items

☐☐☐ Pilot qualifications
☐☐☐ Operation of airplane systems
☐☐☐ Preflight assessment
☐☐☐ Engine starting
☐☐☐ Taxiing
☐☐☐ Runway incursion avoidance
☐☐☐ Before takeoff check
☐☐☐ Radio communication
☐☐☐ Traffic patterns
☐☐☐ Airport markings and signs
☐☐☐ Normal and crosswind takeoff and climb
☐☐☐ Flight by reference to instruments (IR)
☐☐☐ Maneuvering during slow flight

☐☐☐ Power-off stalls (entered from straight flight and turns)
☐☐☐ Power-on stalls (entered from straight flight and turns)
☐☐☐ Steep turns
☐☐☐ Normal and crosswind approach and landing
☐☐☐ Go-around/rejected landing
☐☐☐ Forward slip to a landing
☐☐☐ Recovery from bouncing and ballooning during landing
☐☐☐ ATC light signals
☐☐☐ Additional items at CFI's discretion _____
_____
_____

4. Postflight critique and preview of next lesson

Completion Standards

The lesson will have been successfully completed when the student displays the ability to perform all of the maneuvers safely, without instructor assistance, in preparation for solo flight in the local practice area. At no time will the successful outcome of each task be in doubt.

Instructor's comments:_____

_____

Lesson assignment:_____

_____

Notes:_____

_____

_____

_____

_____

_____

_____

_____

_____

FLIGHT LESSON 10: PRESOLO REVIEW

Objective

The instructor will evaluate and correct any deficiency in the student's performance of the presolo maneuvers in preparation for solo flight.

Content

1. Flight Lesson 9 complete? Yes ___   Copy of lesson placed in student's folder? Yes ___
2. Preflight briefing
3. Review items

☐☐☐ Use of checklists
☐☐☐ Flight deck management
☐☐☐ Normal and crosswind takeoff and climb
☐☐☐ Wake turbulence avoidance
☐☐☐ Collision and obstacle avoidance and scanning
☐☐☐ Wind shear avoidance
☐☐☐ Emergency descent
☐☐☐ Emergency approach and landing
☐☐☐ Systems and equipment malfunctions
☐☐☐ S-turns
☐☐☐ Turns around a point

☐☐☐ Traffic patterns
☐☐☐ Normal and crosswind approach and landing
☐☐☐ Dealing with unexpected requests from ATC (if appropriate)
☐☐☐ Forward slip to a landing
☐☐☐ Go-around/rejected landing
☐☐☐ After landing procedures
☐☐☐ Parking and securing procedures
☐☐☐ Additional items at CFI's discretion _____
_____
_____

4. Postflight critique and preview of next lesson

Completion Standards

The lesson will have been successfully completed when the student displays the ability to perform all of the maneuvers safely, without instructor assistance, in preparation for solo flight in the local practice area. At no time will the successful outcome of each task be in doubt.

Instructor's comments: _____

_____

Lesson assignment: _____

_____

Notes: _____

FLIGHT LESSON 11: FIRST SOLO

Objective

To develop the student's proficiency to a level that will allow the safe accomplishment of the first supervised solo in the traffic pattern.

Text References

Private Pilot Flight Maneuvers and Practical Test Prep (FM)
Pilot Handbook (PH)

Content

1. Flight Lesson 10 complete? Yes ____   Copy of lesson and presolo knowledge test placed in student's folder? Yes ____

2. Preflight briefing
    ☐☐☐ Presolo knowledge test - CFI
    ☐☐☐ Instructor endorsements - CFI
    _____

3. Review items (dual)
    ☐☐☐ Radio communication
    ☐☐☐ Wake turbulence avoidance
    ☐☐☐ Normal and crosswind takeoff and climb
    ☐☐☐ Traffic patterns
    ☐☐☐ Normal and crosswind approach and landing
    ☐☐☐ Go-around/rejected landing
    _____

4. New items (solo in traffic pattern)
    ☐☐☐ Radio communication - FM 16; PH 3
    ☐☐☐ Traffic patterns - FM 17; PH 3
    ☐☐☐ Normal and crosswind takeoff and climb (3) - FM 18
    ☐☐☐ Normal and crosswind approach and landing to a full stop (3) - FM 19
    ☐☐☐ After landing, parking, and securing procedures - FM 47
    ☐☐☐ Additional items at CFI's discretion _____
    _____

5. Postflight critique and preview of next lesson

Completion Standards

The lesson will have been successfully completed when the student completes the presolo knowledge test satisfactorily and safely accomplishes the first supervised solo in the traffic pattern.

Instructor's comments:_____

_____

Lesson assignment:_____

_____

Notes:_____

_____

_____

_____

FLIGHT LESSON 12: STAGE ONE CHECK

Objective

During this stage check, an authorized flight instructor will determine if the student can safely conduct solo flights to the practice area and exercise the privileges associated with the solo operation of the airplane.

Content

1. Flight Lesson 11 complete? Yes ___   Copy of lesson placed in student's folder? Yes ___
2. Preflight briefing
3. Stage check tasks

☐☐☐ Operation of airplane systems
☐☐☐ Preflight assessment
☐☐☐ Flight deck management
☐☐☐ Engine starting
☐☐☐ Radio communication
☐☐☐ Taxiing
☐☐☐ Runway incursion avoidance
☐☐☐ Before takeoff check
☐☐☐ Wake turbulence avoidance
☐☐☐ Normal and crosswind takeoff and climb
☐☐☐ Collision and obstacle avoidance and scanning
☐☐☐ Wind shear avoidance
☐☐☐ Flight by reference to instruments (IR)

☐☐☐ Maneuvering during slow flight
☐☐☐ Power-off stalls
☐☐☐ Power-on stalls
☐☐☐ Systems and equipment malfunctions
☐☐☐ Emergency descent
☐☐☐ Emergency approach and landing
☐☐☐ Traffic patterns
☐☐☐ Normal and crosswind approach and landing
☐☐☐ Go-around/rejected landing
☐☐☐ After landing, parking, and securing procedures
☐☐☐ Additional items at CFI's discretion _____

4. Postflight critique and preview of next lesson

Completion Standards

The lesson and Stage One will have been successfully completed when the student is competent to conduct safe solo flights at the local airport and in the practice area. The student will maintain altitude, ±150 ft.; airspeed, ±10 kt.; and heading, ±20°.

Instructor's comments: _____

Lesson assignment: _____

Notes: _____

STAGE TWO

Stage Two Objective

The student will be introduced to soft- and short-field takeoffs and landings and night-flying operations. Additionally, the student will be instructed in the conduct of cross-country flights in an airplane using pilotage, dead reckoning, and navigation systems while operating under VFR within the U.S. National Airspace System. Finally, the student will receive instruction in preparation for the private pilot (airplane single-engine land) practical test.

Stage Two Completion Standards

The stage will be completed when the student demonstrates proficiency in soft- and short-field takeoffs and landings. Additionally, the student will demonstrate the ability to conduct night flights safely and plan and safely conduct solo cross-country flights in an airplane using pilotage, dead reckoning, and navigation systems while operating under VFR. Finally, the student will have a thorough understanding of aeronautical decision making and risk management while demonstrating proficiency in all tasks of the private pilot airplane (single-engine land) practical test and meet or exceed the minimum acceptable standards for the private pilot certificate.

Lesson	Topic
13	Second Solo
14	Short-Field and Soft-Field Takeoffs and Landings
15	Solo Maneuvers Review
16	Navigation Systems
17	Dual Cross-Country
18	Night Flight -- Local
19	Night Cross-Country
20	Solo Cross-Country (Part 61/141)
20A	Solo Cross-Country (Part 61)
20B	Solo Cross-Country or Local Flight (Part 61)
21	Maneuvers Review
22	Solo Practice
23	Maneuvers Review
24	Solo Practice
25	Stage Two Check
26	End of Course Test

FLIGHT LESSON 13: SECOND SOLO

Objective

To review previous lessons and to accomplish the student's second supervised solo in the traffic pattern.

Content

1. Flight Lesson 12 complete? Yes ___   Copy of lesson placed in student's folder? Yes ___
2. Preflight briefing
3. Review items (dual)
   - ☐☐☐ Normal and crosswind takeoff and climb
   - ☐☐☐ Emergency approach and landing
   - ☐☐☐ S-turns
   - ☐☐☐ Turns around a point
   - ☐☐☐ Normal and crosswind approach and landing
   - ☐☐☐ Forward slip to a landing
   - ☐☐☐ Go-around/rejected landing
   _____

4. Review items (second solo in traffic pattern)
   - ☐☐☐ Radio communication
   - ☐☐☐ Normal and/or crosswind takeoff and climb (3)
   - ☐☐☐ Traffic patterns
   - ☐☐☐ Normal and crosswind approach and landing (3 to full stop)
   - ☐☐☐ After landing, parking, and securing procedures
   - ☐☐☐ Additional items at CFI's discretion _____
   _____

5. Postflight critique and preview of next lesson

Completion Standards

The lesson will have been successfully completed when the student demonstrates solo competence in the maneuvers performed and safely accomplishes the second supervised solo in the traffic pattern. The student will maintain altitude, ±150 ft.; airspeed, ±10 kt.; and heading, ±10°.

Instructor's comments:_____

_____

Lesson assignment:_____

_____

Notes:_____

_____

_____

_____

_____

_____

_____

FLIGHT LESSON 14: SHORT-FIELD AND SOFT-FIELD TAKEOFFS AND LANDINGS

Objective

To introduce the student to the procedures and technique required for short-field and soft-field takeoffs and landings.

Text References

Private Pilot Flight Maneuvers and Practical Test Prep (FM)

Content

1. Flight Lesson 13 complete? Yes ____   Copy of lesson placed in student's folder? Yes ____
2. Preflight briefing
3. Review items
   - ☐☐☐ Maneuvering during slow flight
   - ☐☐☐ Power-off stalls
   - ☐☐☐ Power-on stalls
   - ☐☐☐ Spin awareness
   - ☐☐☐ Emergency approach and landing
   - ☐☐☐ S-turns
   - ☐☐☐ Turns around a point
   - ☐☐☐ Steep turns
   _____

4. New items
   - ☐☐☐ Soft-field takeoff and climb - FM 20
   - ☐☐☐ Soft-field approach and landing - FM 21
   - ☐☐☐ Short-field takeoff and maximum performance climb - FM 22
   - ☐☐☐ Short-field approach and landing - FM 23
   - ☐☐☐ Additional items at CFI's discretion _____
   _____

5. Postflight critique and preview of next lesson

Completion Standards

The lesson will have been successfully completed when the student can explain when it would be necessary to use short-field or soft-field takeoff and landing procedures. Additionally, the student will be able to demonstrate an understanding of these procedures. The student will maintain the desired altitude, ±150 ft.; airspeed, ±10 kt.; and heading, ±10°.

Instructor's comments:_____

_____

Lesson assignment:_____

_____

Notes:_____

_____

_____

_____

_____

_____

FLIGHT LESSON 15: SOLO MANEUVERS REVIEW

Objective

To develop the student's confidence and proficiency through solo practice of assigned maneuvers.

Content

1. Flight Lesson 14 complete? Yes ___   Copy of lesson placed in student's folder? Yes ___
2. Preflight briefing
3. Review items
   - ☐☐☐ Normal and crosswind takeoff and climb
   - ☐☐☐ Maneuvering during slow flight
   - ☐☐☐ Power-off stalls
   - ☐☐☐ Power-on stalls
   - ☐☐☐ Steep turns
   - ☐☐☐ S-turns
   - ☐☐☐ Turns around a point
   - ☐☐☐ Normal and crosswind approach and landing
   - ☐☐☐ Additional items at CFI's discretion _____
   _____
4. Postflight critique and preview of next lesson

Completion Standards

The lesson will have been successfully completed when the student completes the listed maneuvers assigned for the solo flight. The student will gain confidence and proficiency as a result of the solo practice.

Instructor's comments:_____

_____

Lesson assignment:_____

_____

Notes:_____

_____

_____

_____

_____

_____

_____

_____

_____

_____

_____

_____

FLIGHT LESSON 16: NAVIGATION SYSTEMS

Objective

To introduce the student to the proper use of the navigation system(s) installed in the airplane to determine position and track a specified course. Additionally, the student is introduced to more maneuvers while controlling the airplane with reference to the instruments.

Text References

Private Pilot Flight Maneuvers and Practical Test Prep (FM)
Pilot Handbook (PH)
Navigation equipment operation manual(s)

Content

1. Flight Lesson 15 complete? Yes ___   Copy of lesson placed in student's folder? Yes ___
2. Preflight briefing
3. Review items

☐☐☐ Soft-field takeoff and climb   ☐☐☐ Power-off stalls
☐☐☐ Maneuvering during slow flight   ☐☐☐ Power-on stalls
                                           ☐☐☐ Soft-field approach and landing

4. New items

☐☐☐ VOR orientation and tracking - FM 29; PH 10   ☐☐☐ Recovery from unusual flight attitudes (IR) - FM 40
☐☐☐ ADF orientation and tracking - PH 10   ☐☐☐ Radio communications, navigation systems/facilities, and radar services (IR) - FM 41
☐☐☐ GPS orientation and tracking - FM 29; PH 10   ☐☐☐ Additional items at CFI's discretion _____
☐☐☐ Maneuvering during slow flight (IR) - FM 32, 36-39
☐☐☐ Power-off stalls (IR) - FM 33
☐☐☐ Power-on stalls (IR) - FM 34

5. Postflight critique and preview of next lesson

Completion Standards

The lesson will have been successfully completed when the student displays an understanding of the navigation system(s) in the airplane. Additionally, the student will use the correct recovery procedure from unusual attitudes and will be able to maintain control of the airplane by instrument reference and by the use of navigation systems, radio communications, and radar services. All approaches will be stabilized, and the student will maintain the desired airspeed, +10/–5 kt.

Instructor's comments:_____

_____

Lesson assignment:_____

_____

Notes:_____

_____

_____

_____

_____

FLIGHT LESSON 17: DUAL CROSS-COUNTRY

Objective

To introduce the student to cross-country procedures that include flight planning, pilotage and dead reckoning, navigation systems, diversion to an alternate airport, and lost procedures.

Text References

Private Pilot Flight Maneuvers and Practical Test Prep (FM)   Sectional chart
Pilot Handbook (PH)   Chart Supplement
Pilot's Operating Handbook (POH)

Content

1. Flight Lesson 16 complete? Yes ___   Copy of lesson placed in student's folder? Yes ___
2. Preflight briefing
3. Review items

☐☐☐ Navigation systems/facilities   ☐☐☐ Short-field takeoffs and landings
☐☐☐ Emergency descent   ☐☐☐ Soft-field takeoffs and landings
☐☐☐ Emergency approach and landing   ☐☐☐ Forward slip to a landing
☐☐☐ Systems and equipment malfunctions   ☐☐☐ Wind shear avoidance
☐☐☐ Emergency equipment and survival gear   ☐☐☐ Wake turbulence avoidance

4. New items

☐☐☐ Aeronautical charts - PH 9   ☐☐☐ VFR radar services, as appropriate - FM 29; PH 3
☐☐☐ Chart Supplement, Notice to Airmen (NOTAM), and other publications - PH 9   ☐☐☐ Setting power and fuel mixture - POH 4, 5
☐☐☐ National Airspace System - PH 3   ☐☐☐ Estimating in-flight visibility - CFI
☐☐☐ Route selection - FM 6; PH 11   ☐☐☐ Operational problems associated with varying terrain features during the flight - CFI
☐☐☐ Navigation log - PH 11   ☐☐☐ Recognition of critical weather situations - CFI
☐☐☐ Obtaining weather information - FM 5; PH 8   ☐☐☐ Computing groundspeed, ETA, and fuel consumption - PH 9
☐☐☐ Determining performance and limitations - FM 8; PH 5; POH 2, 5   ☐☐☐ Obtaining in-flight weather information - PH 8
☐☐☐ Flight deck management - FM 12   ☐☐☐ Unfamiliar airport operations - CFI
☐☐☐ Weight and balance computations - PH 5; POH 6   ☐☐☐ Lost procedures - FM 31; PH 11
☐☐☐ Human factors - FM 10; PH 6   ☐☐☐ Diversion to an alternate airport - FM 30; PH 11
☐☐☐ Filing a VFR flight plan - PH 11; CFI   ☐☐☐ Closing a VFR flight plan - PH 11; CFI
☐☐☐ Course interception - FM 29   ☐☐☐ Additional items at CFI's discretion _____
☐☐☐ Open VFR flight plan - CFI
☐☐☐ Pilotage and dead reckoning - FM 28; PH 11

5. Postflight critique and preview of next lesson

Completion Standards

The lesson will have been successfully completed when the student, with instructor assistance, is able to perform the cross-country flight planning and fly the planned course making necessary off-course corrections and computing groundspeed, ETA, and fuel consumption. The student will display the ability to navigate by means of pilotage and dead reckoning and by any other navigation system. Additionally, the student will understand how to perform lost procedures and a diversion to an alternate airport.

Instructor's comments:_____

Lesson assignment:_____

Notes:_____

_____

_____

FLIGHT LESSON 18: NIGHT FLIGHT -- LOCAL

Objective

To introduce the student to night-flying preparation and night-flying operations.

Text References

Private Pilot Flight Maneuvers and Practical Test Prep (FM)
Pilot Handbook (PH)
Pilot's Operating Handbook (POH)

Content

1. Flight Lesson 17 complete? Yes ___   Copy of lesson placed in student's folder? Yes ___
2. Preflight briefing
3. New items

☐☐☐ Human factors associated with night flying - PH 6
☐☐☐ Airport lighting - PH 3
☐☐☐ Airplane equipment and lighting requirements - FM 46
☐☐☐ Personal equipment and preparation - FM 46
☐☐☐ Safety precautions while on the ground and in the air - FM 46
☐☐☐ Emergency procedures at night - FM 46
☐☐☐ Night preflight assessment - FM 18, 46
☐☐☐ Flight deck management - FM 12
☐☐☐ Engine starting - FM 13
☐☐☐ Taxiing - FM 14
☐☐☐ Runway incursion avoidance - FM 14; PH 3
☐☐☐ Before takeoff check - FM 15
☐☐☐ Normal takeoffs and landings - FM 18, 46
☐☐☐ Soft-field takeoffs and landings - FM 20-21, 46

☐☐☐ Short-field takeoffs and landings - FM 22-23, 46
☐☐☐ Traffic patterns - FM 17; PH 3
☐☐☐ Go-around/rejected landing - FM 25
☐☐☐ Collision and obstacle avoidance and scanning - PH 3
☐☐☐ Steep turns - FM 26; PH 1
☐☐☐ Maneuvering during slow flight - FM 32; PH 1
☐☐☐ Power-off stalls - FM 33; PH 1
☐☐☐ Power-on stalls - FM 34; PH 1
☐☐☐ Recovery from unusual flight attitudes (IR) - FM 40
☐☐☐ Systems and equipment malfunctions - FM 44; POH 3
☐☐☐ Emergency approach and landing - FM 43; POH 3
☐☐☐ Additional items at CFI's discretion _____

4. Postflight critique and preview of next lesson

Completion Standards

The lesson will have been successfully completed when the student displays the ability to maintain orientation in the local practice area and airport traffic pattern, and can accurately interpret aircraft and airport lights. The student will maintain altitude, ±150 ft.; airspeed, ±10 kt.; and heading, ±10°.

Instructor's comments: _____

_____

Lesson assignment: _____

_____

Notes: _____

_____

_____

_____

FLIGHT LESSON 19: NIGHT CROSS-COUNTRY

Objective

To develop the student's ability to plan and fly a night cross-country flight of more than 100 NM total distance with at least one landing at an unfamiliar airport; to develop the student's proficiency in navigating at night by means of pilotage, dead reckoning, and other navigation system(s).

Text References

Private Pilot Flight Maneuvers and Practical Test Prep (FM)   Sectional chart
Pilot Handbook (PH)   Chart Supplement

Content

1. Flight Lesson 18 complete? Yes ____   Copy of lesson placed in student's folder? Yes ____
2. Preflight briefing
3. Review items

    ☐☐☐ Human factors
    ☐☐☐ Personal equipment and preparation
    ☐☐☐ Obtaining weather information
    ☐☐☐ Determining performance and limitations
    ☐☐☐ Short-field takeoffs and landings
    ☐☐☐ Soft-field takeoffs and landings
    ☐☐☐ Go-around/rejected landing
    ☐☐☐ Straight-and-level flight (IR)
    ☐☐☐ Turns to headings (IR)

    ☐☐☐ Constant airspeed descent and climb (IR)
    ☐☐☐ Navigation systems and ATC services (IR)
    ☐☐☐ Collision and obstacle avoidance and scanning
    ☐☐☐ Pilotage and dead reckoning
    ☐☐☐ Navigation systems
    ☐☐☐ Unfamiliar airport operations
    ☐☐☐ Lost procedures
    ☐☐☐ Diversion to an alternate airport

4. New items

    ☐☐☐ Route selection - FM 6
    ☐☐☐ Night VFR fuel requirements (14 CFR 91.151) - PH 4

    ☐☐☐ Additional items at CFI's discretion _____
    _____
    _____

5. Postflight critique and preview of next lesson
    ☐ Instructor endorse logbook for solo cross-country

Completion Standards

The lesson will have been successfully completed when the student demonstrates the proficiency to conduct safe solo cross-country flights. The student will maintain altitude, ±200 ft.; airspeed, ±10 kt.; established heading, ±15°; and remain within 3 NM of the planned route at all times. Additionally, at the completion of this lesson, the student will have a total of at least 3 hr. of night flight training and 10 takeoffs and 10 landings to a full stop in the traffic pattern. The instructor will endorse the student's logbook for cross-country privileges.

Instructor's comments: _____

_____

Lesson assignment: _____

_____

Notes: _____

_____

_____

FLIGHT LESSON 20: SOLO CROSS-COUNTRY (PART 61/141)

Objective

To increase the student's confidence and proficiency in the conduct of cross-country flights. This solo cross-country flight should be at least 100 NM (150 NM for Part 61 students) total distance with full-stop landings at a minimum of three points, and one segment of the flight should consist of a straight-line distance of at least 50 NM between the takeoff and landing locations.

Content

1. Flight Lesson 19 complete? Yes ____   Copy of lesson placed in student's folder? Yes ____
2. Preflight briefing

    ☐ Instructor review of student's cross-country planning - CFI
    ☐ Instructor logbook endorsement - CFI

3. Review items

    ☐☐☐ Obtaining weather information
    ☐☐☐ Cross-country flight planning
    ☐☐☐ Determining performance and limitations
    ☐☐☐ Pilotage and dead reckoning
    ☐☐☐ Navigation systems
    ☐☐☐ Computing groundspeed, ETA, and fuel
          consumption

    ☐☐☐ Short-field takeoffs and landings
    ☐☐☐ Soft-field takeoffs and landings
    ☐☐☐ Landing at a minimum of three airports
    ☐☐☐ Additional items at CFI's discretion _____
    _____
    _____

4. Postflight critique and preview of next lesson

Completion Standards

The lesson will have been successfully completed when the student can properly plan and conduct the solo cross-country flight using pilotage, dead reckoning, and navigation systems. During the postflight critique, the instructor will determine how well the flight was conducted through oral questioning. The student will have made at least three (3) takeoffs and landings to a full stop at an airport with an operating control tower by the end of this lesson.

Instructor's comments:_____

_____

Lesson assignment:_____

_____

Notes:_____

_____

_____

_____

_____

_____

_____

_____

_____

_____

FLIGHT LESSON 20A: SOLO CROSS-COUNTRY (PART 61)

Objective

To increase the student's proficiency in the conduct of solo cross-country flights. A landing must be conducted at an airport that is at a straight-line distance of more than 50 NM from the original departure airport.

Content

1. Flight Lesson 20 complete? Yes ___   Copy of lesson placed in student's folder? Yes ___
2. Preflight briefing
    - ☐ Instructor review of student's cross-country planning - CFI
    - ☐ Instructor logbook endorsement - CFI
3. Review items
    - ☐☐☐ Obtaining weather information
    - ☐☐☐ Cross-country flight planning
    - ☐☐☐ Determining performance and limitations
    - ☐☐☐ Short-field takeoffs and landings
    - ☐☐☐ Soft-field takeoffs and landings
    - ☐☐☐ Pilotage and dead reckoning
    - ☐☐☐ Navigation systems/facilities and radar services
    - ☐☐☐ Computing groundspeed, ETAs, and fuel consumption
    - ☐☐☐ Tower and/or nontower airport operations
    - ☐☐☐ Landing at an airport more than 50 NM from airport of departure
    - ☐☐☐ Additional items at CFI's discretion _____
4. Postflight critique and preview of next lesson

Completion Standards

The lesson will have been successfully completed when the student completes this cross-country flight as planned. During the postflight critique, the instructor will determine how well the flight was conducted through oral questioning.

Instructor's comments:_____

_____

Lesson assignment:_____

_____

Notes:_____

_____

FLIGHT LESSON 20B: SOLO CROSS-COUNTRY OR LOCAL FLIGHT (PART 61)

Objective

To increase the student's confidence in the conduct of solo cross-country flights.

NOTE: In the event 40 hours of total time is an objective, 1 hour of solo practice may be substituted for this 2-hour cross-country flight.

Content

1. Flight Lesson 20A complete? Yes ___ Copy of lesson placed in student's folder? Yes ___
2. Preflight briefing
   - ☐ Instructor review of student's cross-country planning - CFI
   - ☐ Instructor logbook endorsement - CFI

3. Review items
   - ☐☐☐ Obtaining weather information
   - ☐☐☐ Cross-country flight planning
   - ☐☐☐ Determining performance and limitations
   - ☐☐☐ Pilotage and dead reckoning
   - ☐☐☐ Navigation systems/facilities and radar services
   - ☐☐☐ Computing groundspeed, ETAs, and fuel consumption
   - ☐☐☐ Short-field takeoffs and landings
   - ☐☐☐ Soft-field takeoffs and landings
   - ☐☐☐ Landing at an airport more than 50 NM from airport of departure
   - ☐☐☐ Additional items at CFI's discretion _____
   _____
   _____

4. Postflight critique and preview of next lesson

Completion Standards

The lesson will have been successfully completed when the student completes this cross-country flight as planned. During the postflight critique, the instructor will determine how well the flight was conducted through oral questioning. At completion of this lesson, the student will have at least 5 hr. of solo cross-country flight time.

Instructor's comments: _____

_____

Lesson assignment: _____

_____

Notes: _____

_____

_____

_____

_____

_____

_____

_____

_____

_____

FLIGHT LESSON 21: MANEUVERS REVIEW

Objective

To determine the student's proficiency level in the maneuvers and procedures covered previously.

Content

1. Flight Lesson 20/20A/20B (as appropriate) complete? Yes ____

    Copy of lesson(s) placed in student's folder? Yes ____

2. Preflight briefing

3. Review items

☐☐☐ Airplane logbook entries
    ☐☐☐ Airworthiness requirements
☐☐☐ Operation of airplane systems
☐☐☐ Preflight assessment
☐☐☐ Flight deck management
☐☐☐ Engine starting
☐☐☐ Radio communication
☐☐☐ Airport markings, signs, and lights
☐☐☐ Taxiing
☐☐☐ Runway incursion avoidance
☐☐☐ Before takeoff check
☐☐☐ Short-field takeoff and climb
☐☐☐ Soft-field takeoff and climb
☐☐☐ Steep turns
☐☐☐ Maneuvering during slow flight

☐☐☐ Power-off stalls
☐☐☐ Power-on stalls
☐☐☐ Spin awareness
☐☐☐ Emergency descent
☐☐☐ Emergency approach and landing
☐☐☐ Systems and equipment malfunctions
☐☐☐ Traffic patterns
☐☐☐ Short-field approach and landing
☐☐☐ Soft-field approach and landing
☐☐☐ Go-around/rejected landing
☐☐☐ Forward slip to a landing
☐☐☐ After landing procedures
☐☐☐ Parking and securing the airplane
☐☐☐ Additional items at CFI's discretion _____

_____

_____

4. Postflight critique and preview of next lesson

Completion Standards

The lesson will have been successfully completed when the student demonstrates improved proficiency in the various tasks given. The student will maintain the altitude, airspeed, and heading standards specified for the appropriate task in the current FAA Private Pilot Airman Certification Standards.

Instructor's comments:_____

_____

Lesson assignment:_____

_____

Notes:_____

_____

_____

_____

_____

_____

_____

FLIGHT LESSON 22: SOLO PRACTICE

Objective

To further develop the student's proficiency through solo practice of assigned maneuvers.

Content

1. Flight Lesson 21 complete? Yes ____   Copy of lesson placed in student's folder? Yes ____
2. Preflight briefing
3. Review items
   - ☐☐☐ Short-field takeoffs and landings
   - ☐☐☐ Soft-field takeoffs and landings
   - ☐☐☐ Steep turns
   - ☐☐☐ Maneuvering during slow flight
   - ☐☐☐ Power-on stalls
   - ☐☐☐ Power-off stalls
   - ☐☐☐ Traffic patterns
   - ☐☐☐ Forward slip to a landing
   - ☐☐☐ Radio communication
   - ☐☐☐ Additional items at CFI's discretion _____
   _____

4. Postflight critique and preview of next lesson

Completion Standards

The lesson will have been successfully completed when the student completes the solo flight. The student will gain confidence and improve performance as a result of the solo practice period.

Instructor's comments: _____

_____

Lesson assignment: _____

_____

Notes: _____

_____

_____

_____

_____

_____

_____

_____

_____

_____

_____

_____

FLIGHT LESSON 23: MANEUVERS REVIEW

Objective

To develop improved performance and proficiency in the procedures and maneuvers covered previously.

Content

1. Flight Lesson 22 complete? Yes ___   Copy of lesson placed in student's folder? Yes ___
2. Preflight briefing
3. Review items

☐☐☐ Short-field takeoff and climb
☐☐☐ Soft-field takeoff and climb
☐☐☐ Cross-country procedures
☐☐☐ Maneuvering during slow flight
☐☐☐ Power-off stalls
☐☐☐ Power-on stalls
☐☐☐ Spin awareness
☐☐☐ Straight-and-level flight (IR)
☐☐☐ Turns to headings (IR)
☐☐☐ Constant airspeed descents (IR)
☐☐☐ Constant airspeed climbs (IR)
☐☐☐ Recovery from unusual flight attitudes (IR)
☐☐☐ Radio communications, navigation systems/ facilities, and radar services (IR)

☐☐☐ Emergency approach and landing
☐☐☐ S-turns
☐☐☐ Turns around a point
☐☐☐ Traffic patterns
☐☐☐ Short-field approach and landing
☐☐☐ Soft-field approach and landing
☐☐☐ Go-around/rejected landing
☐☐☐ Forward slip to a landing
☐☐☐ After landing, parking, and securing procedures
☐☐☐ Additional items at CFI's discretion _____

4. Postflight critique and preview of next lesson

Completion Standards

The lesson will have been successfully completed when the student demonstrates improved proficiency in the maneuvers given. The student will complete each task to the standards specified in the current FAA Private Pilot Airman Certification Standards.

Instructor's comments:_____

Lesson assignment:_____

Notes:_____

FLIGHT LESSON 24: SOLO PRACTICE

Objective

To further develop the student's proficiency of assigned maneuvers through solo practice.

Content

1. Flight Lesson 23 complete? Yes ___   Copy of lesson placed in student's folder? Yes ___
2. Preflight briefing
3. Review items
   - ☐☐☐ Short-field takeoffs and landings
   - ☐☐☐ Soft-field takeoffs and landings
   - ☐☐☐ Maneuvering during slow flight
   - ☐☐☐ Power-off stalls
   - ☐☐☐ Power-on stalls
   - ☐☐☐ Steep turns
   - ☐☐☐ S-turns
   - ☐☐☐ Turns around a point
   - ☐☐☐ Traffic patterns
   - ☐☐☐ Forward slip to a landing
   - ☐☐☐ Maneuvers assigned by the instructor
   - ☐☐☐ Additional items at CFI's discretion _____

   _____

4. Postflight critique and preview of next lesson

Completion Standards

The lesson will have been successfully completed when the student completes the solo flight. The student will gain confidence and improve performance as a result of the solo practice period.

Instructor's comments:_____

_____

Lesson assignment:_____

_____

Notes:_____

_____

_____

_____

_____

_____

_____

_____

_____

_____

_____

_____

FLIGHT LESSON 25: STAGE TWO CHECK

Objective

The student will be able to demonstrate the required proficiency of a private pilot by utilizing the current FAA Private Pilot Airman Certification Standards.

Content

1. Flight Lesson 24 complete? Yes ___   Copy of lesson placed in student's folder? Yes ___
2. Stage check tasks

☐☐☐ Pilot qualifications
　　☐☐☐ Airworthiness requirements
☐☐☐ Obtaining weather information
☐☐☐ Cross-country flight planning
☐☐☐ National Airspace System
☐☐☐ Determining performance & limitations
☐☐☐ Operation of airplane systems
☐☐☐ Human factors
☐☐☐ Preflight assessment
☐☐☐ Flight deck management
☐☐☐ Engine starting
☐☐☐ Taxiing
☐☐☐ Runway incursion avoidance
☐☐☐ Before takeoff check
☐☐☐ Radio communication and light signals
☐☐☐ Traffic patterns
☐☐☐ Airport markings, signs, and lights
☐☐☐ Normal and crosswind takeoff and climb
☐☐☐ Soft-field takeoff and climb
☐☐☐ Short-field takeoff and climb
☐☐☐ Pilotage and dead reckoning
☐☐☐ Navigation systems/facilities and radar
　　services
☐☐☐ Lost procedures
☐☐☐ Diversion
☐☐☐ Straight-and-level flight (IR)
☐☐☐ Constant airspeed climbs (IR)
☐☐☐ Constant airspeed descents (IR)

☐☐☐ Turns to headings (IR)
☐☐☐ Unusual flight attitudes (IR)
☐☐☐ Radio communications, navigation systems/
　　facilities, and radar services (IR)
☐☐☐ Steep turns
☐☐☐ Systems and equipment malfunctions
☐☐☐ Maneuvering during slow flight
☐☐☐ Power-off stalls
☐☐☐ Power-on stalls
☐☐☐ Spin awareness
☐☐☐ Emergency descent
☐☐☐ Emergency approach & landing
☐☐☐ Rectangular course
☐☐☐ S-turns
☐☐☐ Turns around a point
☐☐☐ Normal and crosswind approach and landing
☐☐☐ Soft-field approach and landing
☐☐☐ Short-field approach and landing
☐☐☐ Forward slip to a landing
☐☐☐ Go-around/rejected landing
☐☐☐ After landing procedures
☐☐☐ Parking and securing the airplane
☐☐☐ Emergency equipment & survival gear
☐☐☐ Night preparation (oral or flight)
☐☐☐ Night operations (oral or flight)
☐☐☐ Additional items at CFI's discretion _____

3. Postflight critique
4. Flight Lesson 25 complete? Yes ___

Completion Standards

The lesson will have been successfully completed when the student demonstrates the required level of proficiency in all tasks of the current FAA Private Pilot Airman Certification Standards. If additional instruction is necessary, the chief flight instructor will assign the additional training.

Instructor's comments:_____

_____

Notes:_____

_____

_____

_____

_____

FLIGHT LESSON 26: END OF COURSE TEST

Objective

The student will be able to demonstrate the required proficiency of a private pilot by utilizing the current FAA Private Pilot Airman Certification Standards.

Content

1. Flight Lesson 25 complete? Yes ___   Copy of lesson placed in student's folder? Yes ___
2. Stage check tasks

☐☐☐ Pilot qualifications
  ☐☐☐ Airworthiness requirements
☐☐☐ Obtaining weather information
☐☐☐ Cross-country flight planning
☐☐☐ National Airspace System
☐☐☐ Determining performance and limitations
☐☐☐ Operation of airplane systems
☐☐☐ Human factors
☐☐☐ Preflight assessment
☐☐☐ Flight deck management
☐☐☐ Engine starting
☐☐☐ Radio communication and light signals
☐☐☐ Taxiing
☐☐☐ Airport markings, signs, and lights
☐☐☐ Runway incursion avoidance
☐☐☐ Before takeoff check
☐☐☐ Wake turbulence avoidance
☐☐☐ Normal and crosswind takeoff and climb
☐☐☐ Normal and crosswind approach and landing
☐☐☐ Collision and obstacle avoidance and scanning
☐☐☐ Wind shear avoidance
☐☐☐ Soft-field takeoff and climb
☐☐☐ Short-field takeoff and climb
☐☐☐ Soft-field approach and landing
☐☐☐ Short-field approach and landing
☐☐☐ Forward slip to a landing
☐☐☐ Go-around/rejected landing

☐☐☐ Pilotage and dead reckoning
☐☐☐ Lost procedures
☐☐☐ Diversion
☐☐☐ Straight-and-level flight (IR)
☐☐☐ Constant airspeed climbs (IR)
☐☐☐ Constant airspeed descents (IR)
☐☐☐ Turns to headings (IR)
☐☐☐ Unusual flight attitudes (IR)
☐☐☐ Navigation systems/facilities and radar services (IR)
☐☐☐ Spin awareness
☐☐☐ Maneuvering during slow flight
☐☐☐ Power-off stalls
☐☐☐ Power-on stalls
☐☐☐ Steep turns
☐☐☐ Systems and equipment malfunctions
☐☐☐ Emergency descent
☐☐☐ Emergency approach & landing
☐☐☐ Traffic patterns
☐☐☐ Rectangular course
☐☐☐ S-turns
☐☐☐ Turns around a point
☐☐☐ After landing procedures
☐☐☐ Parking and securing the airplane
☐☐☐ Emergency equipment & survival gear
☐☐☐ Night preparation (oral or flight)
☐☐☐ Night operations (oral or flight)
☐☐☐ Additional items at CFI's discretion _____

3. Postflight critique
4. Flight Lesson 26 complete? Yes ___
      Copy of lesson and graduation certificate placed in student's folder? Yes ___

Completion Standards

The lesson will have been successfully completed when the student demonstrates the required level of proficiency in all tasks of the current FAA Private Pilot Airman Certification Standards. The student must have completed 3 hr. of flight training in preparation for the practical test within 60 days preceding the date of the test. If additional instruction is necessary, the chief flight instructor will assign the additional training. If the flight is satisfactory, the chief flight instructor will complete the student's training records and issue a graduation certificate.

Instructor's comments:_____

Notes:_____

_____

_____

_____

_____

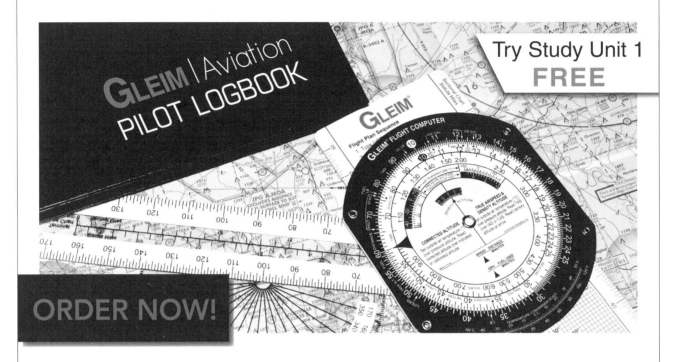

PRESOLO KNOWLEDGE TEST

Airplane make/model: _____

1. List the airspeeds and their definitions for your airplane.

    Airspeed   Definition

    V_{S0} _____   _____

    V_{S1} _____   _____

    V_R _____   _____

    V_X _____   _____

    V_Y _____   _____

    V_{FE} _____   _____

    V_A _____   _____

    V_{NO} _____   _____

    V_{NE} _____   _____

2. The maximum gross weight for your airplane is _____ lb.

3. The maximum takeoff weight for your airplane is _____ lb.

4. Fuel: Maximum capacity _____ gal. of which _____ gal. is usable

    Minimum to start a solo flight _____ gal.

    Grade _____

    Color _____

    Optional grades and colors _____

5. Oil: Maximum capacity _____ qt.

    Minimum to start a solo flight _____ qt.

    Grade _____

6. Compute the location of the center of gravity (CG) for a solo flight with full fuel in your airplane. Is the CG within limits?

7. What is the takeoff ground roll and the distance over a 50-ft. obstacle for your airplane at your airport with full fuel, a temperature of 29°C, 5-kt. headwind, and an altimeter setting of 29.64?

8. What is the ground roll and total landing distance over a 50-ft. obstacle for your airplane at your airport with 3/4 fuel, a temperature of 32°C, calm wind, and an altimeter setting of 30.10?

9. What are the indications of carburetor icing? When is carburetor heat recommended to be used in your airplane?

10. What are the radio frequencies used at your airport?

    Clearance Delivery   _____

    ATIS   _____

    Ground   _____

    Tower   _____

    Approach/Departure   _____

    CTAF   _____

    UNICOM   _____

    FSS   _____

11. At your airport:

    a. What runways are available?

    b. What is the direction of the traffic pattern for each runway?

    c. What is the traffic pattern altitude?

    d. In what class of airspace is the airport located?

12. How do you enter and depart the traffic pattern at your airport?

13. What radio communication procedures are required at your airport?

14. Explain the procedures you would use to land at your airport if the communication radio(s) failed.

15. List the meaning of the following ATC light signals:

	In Flight	On Surface
Steady green	_____	_____
Flashing green	_____	_____
Steady red	_____	_____
Flashing red	_____	_____
Flashing white	_____	_____
Alternating red and green	_____	_____

16. What airplane certificates and documents must be on board the aircraft prior to every flight?

17. What personal documents and endorsements must you have before beginning a solo flight?

18. Who is directly responsible and is the final authority as to the operation of your airplane when you are flying solo?

19. You may not fly as a pilot within _____ hours after the consumption of an alcoholic beverage or with _____ % by weight or more alcohol in the blood.

20. Explain the regulatory preflight action requirements.

21. Explain your use of safety belts and shoulder harnesses while flying solo.

22. When aircraft are approaching each other head-on, or nearly so, what action should be taken?

23. Except for takeoff or landing, at what minimum safe altitudes should you operate your airplane?

24. Explain the altimeter setting procedures.

25. When practicing steep turns, slow flight, power-on stalls, and power-off stalls, you should select an altitude that allows the maneuver to be completed no lower than _____.

26. Explain the go-around procedures in your airplane. When would you use the go-around procedures?

27. The best glide airspeed for your airplane (at maximum gross weight) is _____.

    a.   What airplane configuration is specific to obtain the maximum glide?

28. Explain the actions you would take if the airplane engine failed in the following situations:

    a.   Right after liftoff

    b.   During the takeoff climb at an altitude of 100 ft. AGL

    c.   En route

29. Explain the recommended use of flaps for takeoff in your airplane.

30. For a student pilot, what are the minimum visibility requirements?

31. For a student pilot, what are the restrictions to flight above clouds?

32. For a student pilot, what are the limitations of carrying passengers?

33. What are the day-VFR fuel requirements?

END OF EXAM

STAGE ONE KNOWLEDGE TEST

The figures on pages 77 through 86 are from the FAA's *Airman Knowledge Testing Supplement for Sport Pilot, Recreational Pilot, Remote Pilot, and Private Pilot* book, which is available from your flight school or instructor.

1. An airplane has been loaded in such a manner that the CG is located aft of the aft CG limit. One undesirable flight characteristic a pilot might experience with this airplane would be

A — a longer takeoff run.
B — difficulty in recovering from a stalled condition.
C — stalling at higher-than-normal airspeed.

2. (Refer to Figure 38 on page 83.) Determine the total distance required to land over a 50-foot obstacle.

Pressure altitude = 7,500 ft
Headwind = 8 kts
Temperature = 32°F
Runway = Hard surface

A — 1,004 feet.
B — 1,205 feet.
C — 1,506 feet.

3. (Refer to Figure 40 on page 84.) Determine the approximate ground roll distance required for takeoff.

OAT = 38°C
Pressure altitude = 2,000 ft
Takeoff weight = 2,750 lb
Headwind component = Calm

A — 1,150 feet.
B — 1,300 feet.
C — 1,800 feet.

4. An aircraft is loaded 110 pounds over maximum certificated gross weight. If fuel (gasoline) is drained to bring the aircraft weight within limits, how much fuel should be drained?

A — 15.7 gallons.
B — 16.2 gallons.
C — 18.4 gallons.

5. (Refer to Figure 49 on page 84.) Select the proper traffic pattern and runway for landing.

A — Left-hand traffic and Runway 18.
B — Right-hand traffic and Runway 18.
C — Left-hand traffic and Runway 22.

6. (Refer to Figure 48 on page 85.) What is the difference between area A and area E on the airport depicted?

A — "A" may be used for taxi and takeoff; "E" may be used only as an overrun.
B — "A" may be used for all operations except heavy aircraft landings; "E" may be used only as an overrun.
C — "A" may be used only for taxiing; "E" may be used for all operations except landings.

7. (Refer to Figure 34 on page 82.) Determine the aircraft loaded moment and the aircraft category.

	WEIGHT (LB)	MOM/1000
Empty weight	1,350	51.5
Pilot and front passenger	380	---
Fuel, 48 gal	288	---
Oil, 8 qt.	---	---

A — 78.2, normal category.
B — 79.2, normal category.
C — 80.4, utility category.

8. If a pilot suspects that the engine (with a fixed-pitch propeller) is detonating during climb-out after takeoff, the initial corrective action to take would be to

A — lean the mixture.
B — lower the nose slightly to increase airspeed.
C — apply carburetor heat.

9. After takeoff, which airspeed would the pilot use to gain the most altitude in a given period of time?

A — V_Y.
B — V_X.
C — V_A.

10. What must a pilot be aware of as a result of ground effect?

A — Wingtip vortices increase creating wake turbulence problems for arriving and departing aircraft.
B — Induced drag decreases; therefore, any excess speed at the point of flare may cause considerable floating.
C — A full stall landing will require less up elevator deflection than would a full stall when done free of ground effect.

11. A steady green light signal directed from the control tower to an aircraft in flight is a signal that the pilot

A — is cleared to land.
B — should give way to other aircraft and continue circling.
C — should return for landing.

12. If a flight is made from an area of high pressure into an area of lower pressure without the altimeter setting being adjusted, the altimeter will indicate

A — lower than the actual altitude above sea level.
B — higher than the actual altitude above sea level.
C — the actual altitude above sea level.

13. What change occurs in the fuel/air mixture when carburetor heat is applied?

A — A decrease in RPM results from the lean mixture.
B — The fuel/air mixture becomes richer.
C — The fuel/air mixture becomes leaner.

14. If an aircraft is equipped with a fixed-pitch propeller and a float-type carburetor, the first indication of carburetor ice would most likely be

A — increase of RPM.
B — engine roughness.
C — decrease of RPM.

15. The most effective method of scanning for other aircraft for collision avoidance during daylight hours is to use

A — regularly spaced concentration on the 3-, 9-, and 12-o'clock positions.
B — a series of short, regularly spaced eye movements to search each 10-degree sector.
C — peripheral vision by scanning small sectors and utilizing offcenter viewing.

16. What is the relationship of lift, drag, thrust, and weight when the airplane is in straight-and-level flight?

A — Lift equals weight and thrust equals drag.
B — Lift, drag, and weight equal thrust.
C — Lift and weight equal thrust and drag.

17. In what flight condition must an aircraft be placed in order to spin?

A — Partially stalled with one wing low.
B — In a steep diving spiral.
C — Stalled.

18. During an approach to a stall, an increased load factor will cause the aircraft to

A — stall at a higher airspeed.
B — have a tendency to spin.
C — be more difficult to control.

19. Which instrument(s) will become inoperative if the static vents become clogged?

A — Airspeed indicator only.
B — Altimeter only.
C — Airspeed indicator, altimeter, and vertical speed indicator.

20. What effect does high density altitude, as compared to low density altitude, have on propeller efficiency and why?

A — Efficiency is increased due to less friction on the propeller blades.
B — Efficiency is reduced because the propeller exerts less force at high density altitudes than at low density altitudes.
C — Efficiency is reduced due to the increased force of the propeller in the thinner air.

21. How long does the Airworthiness Certificate of an aircraft remain valid?

A — As long as the aircraft has a current Registration Certificate.
B — Indefinitely, unless the aircraft suffers major damage.
C — As long as the aircraft is maintained and operated as required by Federal Aviation Regulations.

22. If an altimeter setting is not available before flight, to which altitude should the pilot adjust the altimeter?

A — The elevation of the nearest airport corrected to mean sea level.
B — The elevation of the departure area.
C — Pressure altitude corrected for nonstandard temperature.

23. What aircraft inspections are required for rental aircraft that are also used for flight instruction?

A — Annual condition and 100-hour inspections.
B — Biannual condition and 100-hour inspections.
C — Annual condition and 50-hour inspections.

24. Except when necessary for takeoff or landing, what is the minimum safe altitude for a pilot to operate an aircraft anywhere?

A — An altitude allowing, if a power unit fails, an emergency landing without undue hazard to persons or property on the surface.
B — An altitude of 500 feet above the surface and no closer than 500 feet to any person, vessel, vehicle, or structure.
C — An altitude of 500 feet above the highest obstacle within a horizontal radius of 1,000 feet.

25. If instructed by ground control to taxi to Runway 9, the pilot may proceed

A — via taxiways and across runways to, but not onto, Runway 9.

B — to the next intersecting runway where further clearance is required.

C — via taxiways and across runways to Runway 9, where an immediate takeoff may be made.

STAGE TWO KNOWLEDGE TEST

The figures on the inside front and back covers and pages 77 through 86 are from the FAA's *Airman Knowledge Testing Supplement for Sport Pilot, Recreational Pilot, Remote Pilot, and Private Pilot* book, which is available from your flight school or instructor.

1. (Refer to Figure 23 on the inside back cover.) (Refer to Area 3.) What is the floor of the Savannah Class C airspace at the shelf area (outer circle)?

A — 1,200 feet AGL.
B — 1,300 feet MSL.
C — 1,700 feet MSL.

2. (Refer to Figure 12 on page 77.) The wind direction and velocity at KJFK is from

A — 180° true at 4 knots.
B — 180° magnetic at 4 knots.
C — 040° true at 18 knots.

3. Which statement about longitude and latitude is true?

A — Lines of longitude are parallel to the Equator.
B — Lines of longitude cross the Equator at right angles.
C — The 0° line of latitude passes through Greenwich, England.

4. (Refer to Figure 23 on the inside back cover.) The flag symbols at Statesboro Bulloch County Airport, Claxton-Evans County Airport, and Ridgeland Airport are

A — outer boundaries of Savannah Class C airspace.
B — airports with special traffic patterns.
C — visual checkpoints to identify position for initial callup prior to entering Savannah Class C airspace.

5. (Refer to Figure 25 on the inside front cover.) (Refer to Area 3.) If Dallas Executive Tower is not in operation, which frequency should be used as a Common Traffic Advisory Frequency (CTAF) to monitor airport traffic?

A — 127.25 MHz.
B — 122.95 MHz.
C — 126.35 MHz.

6. (Refer to Figure 15 on page 77.) In the TAF from KOKC, the clear sky becomes

A — overcast at 2,000 feet during the forecast period between 2200Z and 2400Z.
B — overcast at 200 feet with a 40 percent probability of becoming overcast at 600 feet during the forecast period between 2200Z and 2400Z.
C — overcast at 200 feet with the probability of becoming overcast at 400 feet during the forecast period between 2200Z and 2400Z.

7. (Refer to Figure 52 on page 86.) Traffic patterns in effect at Lincoln Municipal are

A — to the right on Runway 14 and Runway 32; to the left on Runway 18 and Runway 35.
B — to the left on Runway 14 and Runway 32; to the right on Runway 18 and Runway 35.
C — to the right on Runways 14 - 32.

8. (Refer to Figure 28 on page 79.) (Refer to illustration 8.) The VOR receiver has the indications shown. What is the aircraft's position relative to the station?

A — North.
B — East.
C — South.

9. What is the most effective way to use the eyes during night flight?

A — Look only at far away, dim lights.
B — Scan slowly to permit off-center viewing.
C — Concentrate directly on each object for a few seconds.

10. What minimum radio equipment is required for VFR operation within Class B airspace?

A — Two-way radio communications equipment, a 4096-code transponder, and ADS-B Out equipment.
B — Two-way radio communications equipment, a 4096-code transponder, an encoding altimeter, and ADS-B Out equipment.
C — Two-way radio communications equipment, a 4096-code transponder, an encoding altimeter, ADS-B Out equipment, and a VOR or TACAN receiver.

11. With certain exceptions, Class E airspace extends upward from either 700 feet or 1,200 feet AGL to, but does not include,

A — 10,000 feet MSL.
B — 14,500 feet MSL.
C — 18,000 feet MSL.

12. (Refer to Figure 25 on the inside front cover.) Determine the magnetic heading for a flight from Fort Worth Meacham (area 4) to Denton Muni (area 1). The wind is from 330° at 25 knots, the true airspeed is 110 knots, and the magnetic variation is 7°E.

A — 003°.
B — 017°.
C — 023°.

13. What values are used for Winds Aloft Forecasts?

A — Magnetic direction and knots.
B — Magnetic direction and miles per hour.
C — True direction and knots.

14. What information is contained in a CONVECTIVE SIGMET?

A — Tornadoes, embedded thunderstorms, and hail 3/4 inch or greater in diameter.
B — Severe icing, severe turbulence, or widespread dust storms lowering visibility to less than 3 miles.
C — Surface winds greater than 40 knots or thunderstorms equal to or greater than video integrator processor (VIP) level 4.

15. When the course deviation indicator (CDI) needle is centered using a VOR test signal (VOT), the omnibearing selector (OBS) and the TO/FROM indicator should read

A — 180° FROM, only if the pilot is due north of the VOT.
B — 0° TO or 180° FROM, regardless of the pilot's position from the VOT.
C — 0° FROM or 180° TO, regardless of the pilot's position from the VOT.

16. The angular difference between true north and magnetic north is

A — magnetic deviation.
B — magnetic variation.
C — compass acceleration error.

17. Which of the following is a correct response to counteract the feelings of hypoxia in flight?

A — Promptly descend to a lower altitude.
B — Increase cabin air flow.
C — Avoid sudden inhalations.

18. Pilots are more subject to spatial disorientation if

A — they ignore the sensations of muscles and inner ear.
B — visual cues are taken away, as they are in instrument meteorological conditions (IMC).
C — eyes are moved often in the process of cross-checking the flight instruments.

19. (Refer to Figure 23 on the inside back cover.) What is the approximate position of the aircraft if the VOR receivers indicate the 340°radial of Savannah VORTAC (area 3) and the 184° radial of Allendale VOR (area 1)?

A — Town of Guyton.
B — Town of Springfield.
C — 3 miles east of Briggs.

20. Which conditions result in the formation of frost?

A — The temperature of the collecting surface is at or below freezing when small droplets of moisture fall on the surface.
B — The temperature of the collecting surface is at or below the dewpoint of the adjacent air and the dewpoint is below freezing.
C — The temperature of the surrounding air is at or below freezing when small drops of moisture fall on the collecting surface.

21. What conditions are necessary for the formation of thunderstorms?

A — High humidity, lifting force, and unstable conditions.
B — High humidity, high temperature, and cumulus clouds.
C — Lifting force, moist air, and extensive cloud cover.

22. One weather phenomenon which will always occur when flying across a front is a change in the

A — wind direction.
B — type of precipitation.
C — stability of the air mass.

23. Steady precipitation preceding a front is an indication of

A — stratiform clouds with moderate turbulence.
B — cumuliform clouds with little or no turbulence.
C — stratiform clouds with little or no turbulence.

24. Which type weather briefing should a pilot request, when departing within the hour, if no preliminary weather information has been received?

A — Outlook briefing.
B — Abbreviated briefing.
C — Standard briefing.

25. When may hazardous wind shear be expected?

A — When stable air crosses a mountain barrier where it tends to flow in layers forming lenticular clouds.
B — In areas of low-level temperature inversion, frontal zones, and clear air turbulence.
C — Following frontal passage when stratocumulus clouds form indicating mechanical mixing.

END-OF-COURSE KNOWLEDGE TEST

The figures on the inside front and back covers and pages 77 through 86 are from the FAA's *Airman Knowledge Testing Supplement for Sport Pilot, Recreational Pilot, Remote Pilot, and Private Pilot* book, which is available from your flight school or instructor.

1. (Refer to Figure 8 on page 78.) What is the effect of a temperature increase from 25 to 50° F on the density altitude if the pressure altitude remains at 5,000 feet?

A — 1,200-foot increase.
B — 1,400-foot increase.
C — 1,650-foot increase.

2. (Refer to Figure 40 on page 84.) Determine the total distance required for takeoff to clear a 50-foot obstacle.

OAT = Std
Pressure altitude = 4,000 ft
Takeoff weight = 2,800 lb
Headwind component = Calm

A — 1,500 feet.
B — 1,750 feet.
C — 2,000 feet.

3. (Refer to Figure 23 on the inside back cover.) Determine the magnetic heading for a flight from Allendale County Airport (area 1) to Claxton-Evans County Airport (area 2). The wind is from 090° at 16 knots and the true airspeed is 90 knots. Magnetic variation is 7°W.

A — 230°.
B — 213°.
C — 210°.

4. (Refer to Figure 36 on page 83.) With a reported wind of south at 20 knots, which runway is appropriate for an airplane with a 13-knot maximum crosswind component?

A — Runway 10.
B — Runway 14.
C — Runway 24.

5. If an aircraft is loaded 90 pounds over maximum certificated gross weight and fuel (gasoline) is drained to bring the aircraft weight within limits, how much fuel should be drained?

A — 10 gallons.
B — 12 gallons.
C — 15 gallons.

6. (Refer to Figure 32 on page 80 and Figure 33 on page 81.) Which action can adjust the airplane's weight to maximum gross weight and the CG within limits for takeoff?

Front seat occupants = 425 lb
Rear seat occupants = 300 lb
Fuel, main tanks = 44 gal

A — Drain 12 gallons of fuel.
B — Drain 9 gallons of fuel.
C — Transfer 12 gallons of fuel from the main tanks to the auxiliary tanks.

7. What is true altitude?

A — The vertical distance of the aircraft above sea level.
B — The vertical distance of the aircraft above the surface.
C — The height above the standard datum plane.

8. Radar weather reports are of special interest to pilots because they indicate

A — large areas of low ceilings and fog.
B — location of precipitation along with type, intensity, and cell movement of precipitation.
C — location of precipitation along with type, intensity, and trend.

9. (Refer to Figure 25 on the inside front cover.) (Refer to Area 4.) The airspace directly overlying Fort Worth Meacham is

A — Class B airspace to 10,000 feet MSL.
B — Class C airspace to 5,000 feet MSL.
C — Class D airspace to 3,200 feet MSL.

10. (Refer to Figure 12 on page 77.) Which of the reporting stations have VFR weather?

A — All.
B — KINK, KBOI, and KJFK.
C — KINK, KBOI, and KLAX.

11. (Refer to Figure 14 on page 77.) If the terrain elevation is 1,295 feet MSL, what is the height above ground level of the base of the ceiling?

A — 505 feet AGL.
B — 1,295 feet AGL.
C — 6,586 feet AGL.

12. (Refer to Figure 25 on the inside front cover.) (Refer to Area 3.) The floor of Class B airspace at Dallas Executive Airport is

A — at the surface.
B — 3,000 feet MSL.
C — 3,100 feet MSL.

13. (Refer to Figure 25 on the inside front cover.) (Refer to Area 2.) The control tower frequency for Addison Airport is

A — 122.95 MHz.
B — 126.0 MHz.
C — 133.4 MHz.

14. (Refer to Figure 23 on the inside back cover.) On what course should the VOR receiver (OBS) be set to navigate direct from Hampton Varnville Airport (area 1) to Savannah VORTAC (area 3)?

A — 015°.
B — 195°.
C — 201°.

15. (Refer to Figure 15 on page 77.) The only cloud type forecast in TAF reports is

A — Nimbostratus.
B — Cumulonimbus.
C — Scattered cumulus.

16. (Refer to Figure 4 on page 77.) What is the full flap operating range for the airplane?

A — 55 to 100 kts.
B — 55 to 208 kts.
C — 55 to 165 kts.

17. (Refer to Figure 28 on page 79.) (Refer to illustration 5.) The VOR receiver has the indications shown. What radial is the aircraft crossing?

A — 030°.
B — 210°.
C — 300°.

18. (Refer to Figure 25 on the inside front cover.) (Refer to area 5.) The VOR is tuned to the Dallas/Fort Worth VOR. The omnibearing selector (OBS) is set on 253°, with a TO indication, and a right course deviation indicator (CDI) deflection. What is the aircraft's position from the VOR?

A — East-northeast.
B — North-northeast.
C — West-southwest.

19. (Refer to Figure 28 on page 79.) (Refer to illustration 3.) The VOR receiver has the indications shown. What is the aircraft's position relative to the station?

A — East.
B — Southeast.
C — West.

20. Susceptibility to carbon monoxide poisoning increases as

A — altitude increases.
B — altitude decreases.
C — air pressure increases.

21. Hazardous attitudes occur to every pilot to some degree at some time. What are some of these hazardous attitudes?

A — Antiauthority, impulsivity, macho, resignation, and invulnerability.
B — Poor situational awareness, snap judgments, and lack of a decision making process.
C — Poor risk management and lack of stress management.

22. (Refer to Figure 9 on page 77.) (Refer to area C.) How should the flight controls be held while taxiing a tailwheel airplane with a left quartering tailwind?

A — Left aileron up, elevator neutral.
B — Left aileron down, elevator neutral.
C — Left aileron down, elevator down.

23. Detonation occurs in a reciprocating aircraft engine when

A — the spark plugs are fouled or shorted out or the wiring is defective.
B — hot spots in the combustion chamber ignite the fuel/air mixture in advance of normal ignition.
C — the unburned charge in the cylinders explodes instead of burning normally.

24. During a night flight, you observe a steady red light and a flashing red light ahead and at the same altitude. What is the general direction of movement of the other aircraft?

A — The other aircraft is crossing to the left.
B — The other aircraft is crossing to the right.
C — The other aircraft is approaching head-on.

25. (Refer to Figure 47 on page 84.) Illustration A indicates that the aircraft is

A — below the glide slope.
B — on the glide slope.
C — above the glide slope.

26. What ATC facility should the pilot contact to receive a special VFR departure clearance in Class D airspace?

A — Automated Flight Service Station.
B — Air Traffic Control Tower.
C — Air Route Traffic Control Center.

27. When a control tower located on an airport within Class D airspace ceases operation for the day, what happens to the airspace designation?

A — The airspace designation normally will not change.
B — The airspace remains Class D airspace as long as a weather observer or automated weather system is available.
C — The airspace reverts to Class E or a combination of Class E and G airspace during the hours the tower is not in operation.

28. During operations within controlled airspace at altitudes of less than 1,200 feet AGL, the minimum horizontal distance from clouds requirement for VFR flight is

A — 1,000 feet.
B — 1,500 feet.
C — 2,000 feet.

29. Which condition would cause the altimeter to indicate a lower altitude than true altitude?

A — Air temperature lower than standard.
B — Atmospheric pressure lower than standard.
C — Air temperature warmer than standard.

30. Which condition is most favorable to the development of carburetor icing?

A — Any temperature below freezing and a relative humidity of less than 50 percent.
B — Temperature between 32°F and 50°F and low humidity.
C — Temperature between 20°F and 70°F and high humidity.

31. Prior to starting each maneuver, pilots should

A — check altitude, airspeed, and heading indications.
B — visually scan the entire area for collision avoidance.
C — announce their intentions on the nearest CTAF.

32. What determines the longitudinal stability of an airplane?

A — The location of the CG with respect to the center of lift.
B — The effectiveness of the horizontal stabilizer, rudder, and rudder trim tab.
C — The relationship of thrust and lift to weight and drag.

33. In the Northern Hemisphere, the magnetic compass will normally indicate a turn toward the south when

A — a left turn is entered from an east heading.
B — a right turn is entered from a west heading.
C — the aircraft is decelerated while on a west heading.

34. VFR approaches to land at night should be accomplished

A — at a higher airspeed.
B — with a steeper descent.
C — the same as during daytime.

35. Each pilot of an aircraft approaching to land on a runway served by a visual approach slope indicator (VASI) shall

A — maintain a 3° glide to the runway.
B — maintain an altitude at or above the glide slope.
C — stay high until the runway can be reached in a power-off landing.

36. When are the four forces that act on an airplane in equilibrium?

A — During unaccelerated level flight.
B — When the aircraft is accelerating.
C — When the aircraft is at rest on the ground.

37. What is an important airspeed limitation that is not color coded on airspeed indicators?

A — Never-exceed speed.
B — Maximum structural cruising speed.
C — Maneuvering speed.

38. Which in-flight advisory would contain information on severe icing not associated with thunderstorms?

A — Convective SIGMET.
B — SIGMET.
C — AIRMET.

39. The presence of ice pellets at the surface is evidence that there

A — are thunderstorms in the area.
B — has been cold frontal passage.
C — is a temperature inversion with freezing rain at a higher altitude.

40. Which statement best defines hypoxia?

A — A state of oxygen deficiency in the body.
B — An abnormal increase in the volume of air breathed.
C — A condition of gas bubble formation around the joints or muscles.

41. If the pitot tube and outside static vents become clogged, which instruments would be affected?

A — The altimeter, airspeed indicator, and turn-and-slip indicator.

B — The altimeter, airspeed indicator, and vertical speed indicator.

C — The altimeter, attitude indicator, and turn-and-slip indicator.

42. What action can a pilot take to aid in cooling an engine that is overheating during a climb?

A — Reduce rate of climb and increase airspeed.

B — Reduce climb speed and increase RPM.

C — Increase climb speed and increase RPM.

43. Which incident requires an immediate notification be made to the nearest NTSB field office?

A — An overdue aircraft that is believed to be involved in an accident.

B — An in-flight radio communications failure.

C — An in-flight generator or alternator failure.

44. With respect to the certification of airmen, which are categories of aircraft?

A — Gyroplane, helicopter, airship, free balloon.

B — Airplane, rotorcraft, glider, lighter-than-air.

C — Single-engine land and sea, multiengine land and sea.

45. A 100-hour inspection was due at 3302.5 hours. The 100-hour inspection was actually done at 3309.5 hours. When is the next 100-hour inspection due?

A — 3312.5 hours.

B — 3402.5 hours.

C — 3395.5 hours.

46. Prior to takeoff, the altimeter should be set to which altitude or altimeter setting?

A — The current local altimeter setting, if available, or the departure airport elevation.

B — The corrected density altitude of the departure airport.

C — The corrected pressure altitude for the departure airport.

47. When must a current pilot certificate be in the pilot's personal possession or readily accessible in the aircraft?

A — When acting as a crew chief during launch and recovery.

B — Only when passengers are carried.

C — Any time when acting as pilot in command or as a required crewmember.

48. An airplane and an airship are converging. If the airship is left of the airplane's position, which aircraft has the right-of-way?

A — The airship.

B — The airplane.

C — Each pilot should alter course to the right.

49. As standard operating practice, all inbound traffic to an airport without a control tower should continuously monitor the appropriate facility from a distance of

A — 25 miles.

B — 20 miles.

C — 10 miles.

50. Unless each occupant is provided with supplemental oxygen, no person may operate a civil aircraft of U.S. registry above a maximum cabin pressure altitude of

A — 12,500 feet MSL.

B — 14,000 feet MSL.

C — 15,000 feet MSL.

51. The three takeoffs and landings that are required to act as pilot in command at night must be done during the time period from

A — sunset to sunrise.

B — 1 hour after sunset to 1 hour before sunrise.

C — the end of evening civil twilight to the beginning of morning civil twilight.

52. In regard to privileges and limitations, a private pilot may

A — act as pilot in command of an aircraft carrying a passenger for compensation if the flight is in connection with a business or employment.

B — not pay less than the pro rata share of the operating expenses of a flight with passengers provided the expenses involve only fuel, oil, airport expenditures, or rental fees.

C — not be paid in any manner for the operating expenses of a flight.

53. Under what condition, if any, may a pilot allow a person who is obviously under the influence of drugs to be carried aboard an aircraft?

A — In an emergency or if the person is a medical patient under proper care.

B — Only if the person does not have access to the flight deck or pilot's compartment.

C — Under no condition.

54. What is one purpose of wing flaps?

A — To enable the pilot to make steeper approaches to a landing without increasing the airspeed.
B — To relieve the pilot of maintaining continuous pressure on the controls.
C — To decrease wing area to vary the lift.

55. Thunderstorms reach their greatest intensity during the

A — mature stage.
B — downdraft stage.
C — cumulus stage.

56. A stable air mass is most likely to have which characteristic?

A — Showery precipitation.
B — Turbulent air.
C — Poor surface visibility.

57. Every physical process of weather is accompanied by, or is the result of, a

A — movement of air.
B — pressure differential.
C — heat exchange.

58. When requesting weather information for the following morning, a pilot should request

A — an outlook briefing.
B — a standard briefing.
C — an abbreviated briefing.

59. Convective circulation patterns associated with sea breezes are caused by

A — warm, dense air moving inland from over the water.
B — water absorbing and radiating heat faster than the land.
C — cool, dense air moving inland from over the water.

60. Where does wind shear occur?

A — Only at higher altitudes.
B — Only at lower altitudes.
C — At all altitudes, in all directions.

FIGURES

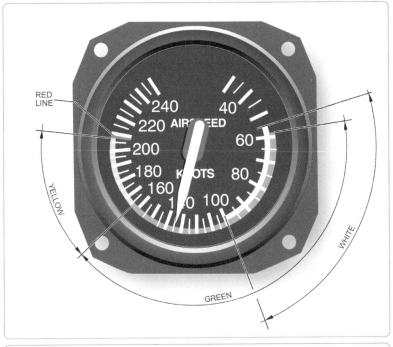

NOTE: Figure 4 is in color in the *FAA Airman Knowledge Testing Supplement for Sport Pilot, Recreational Pilot, Remote Pilot, and Private Pilot,* which you will use during your test.

Figure 4. – Airspeed Indicator.

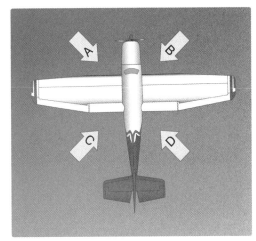

Figure 9. – Control Position for Taxi.

METAR KINK 121845Z 11012G18KT 15SM SKC 25/17 A3000

METAR KBOI 121854Z 13004KT 30SM SCT150 17/6 A3015

METAR KLAX 121852Z 25004KT 6SM BR SCT007 SCT007 SCT250 16/15 A2991

SPECI KMDW 121856Z 32005KT 1 1/2SM RA OVC007 17/16 A2980 RMK RAB35

SPECI KJFK 121853Z 18004KT 1/2SM FG R04/2200 OVC005 20/18 A3006

Figure 12. – Aviation Routine Weather Reports (METAR).

UA/OV KOKC-KTUL/TM 1800/FL 120/TP BE90//SK BKN018-TOP055/OVC072-TOP089/CLR ABV/TA M7/WV 08021/TB LGT 055-072/IC LGT-MOD RIME 072-089

Figure 14. – Pilot Weather Report.

TAF

KMEM 121720Z 121818 20012KT 5SM HZ BKN030 PROB40 2022 1SM TSRA OVC008CB
FM2200 33015G20KT P6SM BKN015 OVC025 PROB40 2202 3SM SHRA
FM0200 35012KT OVC008 PROB40 0205 2SM-RASN BECMG 0608 02008KT BKN012
BECMG 1012 00000KT 3SM BR SKC TEMPO 1214 1/2SM FG
FM1600 VRB06KT P6SM SKC=

KOKC 051130Z 051212 14008KT 5SM BR BKN030 TEMPO 1316 1 1/2SM BR
FM1600 18010KT P6SM SKC BECMG 2224 20013G20KT 4SM SHRA OVC020
PROB40 0006 2SM TSRA OVC008CB BECMG 0608 21015KT P6SM SCT040=

Figure 15. – Terminal Aerodrome Forecasts (TAF).

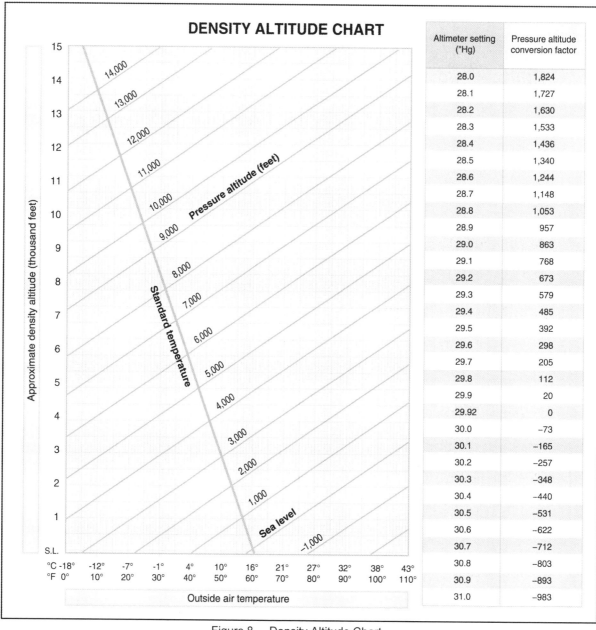

Figure 8. – Density Altitude Chart.

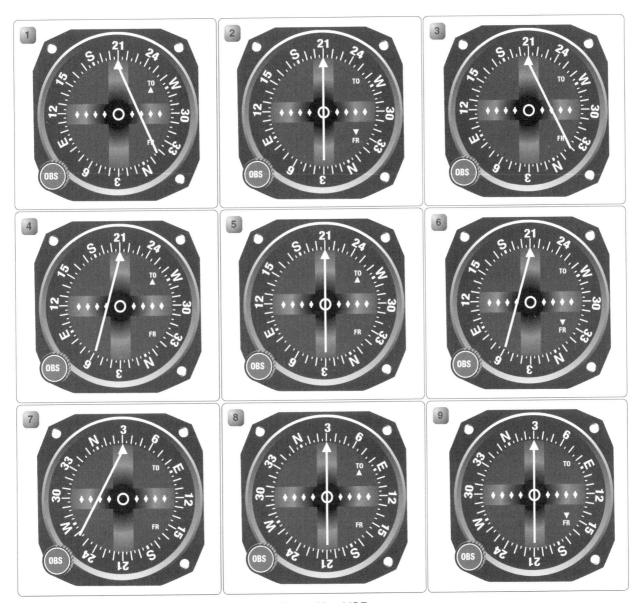

Figure 28. – VOR.

Useful load weights and moments

Baggage or 5th seat occupant

ARM 140

Weight	Moment 100
10	14
20	28
30	42
40	56
50	70
60	84
70	98
80	112
90	126
100	140
110	154
120	168
130	182
140	196
150	210
160	224
170	238
180	252
190	266
200	280
210	294
220	308
230	322
240	336
250	350
260	364
270	378

Occupants

Front seats ARM 85		Rear seats ARM 121	
Weight	Moment 100	Weight	Moment 100
120	102	120	145
130	110	130	157
140	119	140	169
150	128	150	182
160	136	160	194
170	144	170	206
180	153	180	218
190	162	190	230
200	170	200	242

Usable fuel

Main wing tanks ARM 75

Gallons	Weight	Moment 100
5	30	22
10	60	45
15	90	68
20	120	90
25	150	112
30	180	135
35	210	158
40	240	180
44	264	198

Auxiliary wing tanks ARM 94

Gallons	Weight	Moment 100
5	30	28
10	60	56
15	90	85
19	114	107

Empty weight ~2,015

MOM/100 ~1,554

Moment limits vs weight
Moment limits are based on the following weight and center of gravity limit data (landing gear down).

*Oil

Quarts	Weight	Moment 100
10	19	5

*Included in basic empty weight.

Weight condition	Forward CG limit	AFT CG limit
2,950 lb (takeoff or landing)	82.1	84.7
2,525 lb	77.5	85.7
2,475 lb or less	77.0	85.7

Figure 32. – Airplane Weight and Balance Tables.

Weight	Minimum Moment 100	Maximum Moment 100	Weight	Minimum Moment 100	Maximum Moment 100
		Moment limits vs weight (continued)			
2,100	1,617	1,800	2,500	1,932	2,143
2,110	1,625	1,808	2,510	1,942	2,151
2,120	1,632	1,817	2,520	1,953	2,160
2,130	1,640	1,825	2,530	1,963	2,168
2,140	1,648	1,834	2,540	1,974	2,176
2,150	1,656	1,843	2,550	1,984	2,184
2,160	1,663	1,851	2,560	1,995	2,192
2,170	1,671	1,860	2,570	2,005	2,200
2,180	1,679	1,868	2,580	2,016	2,208
2,190	1,686	1,877	2,590	2,026	2,216
2,200	1,694	1,885	2,600	2,037	2,224
2,210	1,702	1,894	2,610	2,048	2,232
2,220	1,709	1,903	2,620	2,058	2,239
2,230	1,717	1,911	2,630	2,069	2,247
2,240	1,725	1,920	2,640	2,080	2,255
2,250	1,733	1,928	2,650	2,090	2,263
2,260	1,740	1,937	2,660	2,101	2,271
2,270	1,748	1,945	2,670	2,112	2,279
2,280	1,756	1,954	2,680	2,123	2,287
2,290	1,763	1,963	2,690	2,133	2,295
2,300	1,771	1,971	2,700	2,144	2,303
2,310	1,779	1,980	2,710	2,155	2,311
2,320	1,786	1,988	2,720	2,166	2,319
2,330	1,794	1,997	2,730	2,177	2,326
2,340	1,802	2,005	2,740	2,188	2,334
2,350	1,810	2,014	2,750	2,199	2,342
2,360	1,817	2,023	2,760	2,210	2,350
2,370	1,825	2,031	2,770	2,221	2,358
2,380	1,833	2,040	2,780	2,232	2,366
2,390	1,840	2,048	2,790	2,243	2,374
2,400	1,848	2,057	2,800	2,254	2,381
2,410	1,856	2,065	2,810	2,265	2,389
2,420	1,863	2,074	2,820	2,276	2,397
2,430	1,871	2,083	2,830	2,287	2,405
2,440	1,879	2,091	2,840	2,298	2,413
2,450	1,887	2,100	2,850	2,309	2,421
2,460	1,894	2,108	2,860	2,320	2,428
2,470	1,902	2,117	2,870	2,332	2,436
2,480	1,911	2,125	2,880	2,343	2,444
2,490	1,921	2,134	2,890	2,354	2,452
			2,900	2,365	2,460
			2,910	2,377	2,468
			2,920	2,388	2,475
			2,930	2,399	2,483
			2,940	2,411	2,491
			2,950	2,422	2,499

Figure 33. – Airplane Weight and Balance Tables.

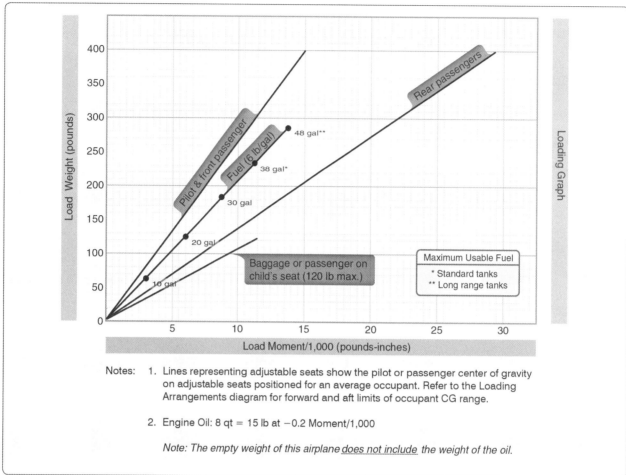

Notes: 1. Lines representing adjustable seats show the pilot or passenger center of gravity on adjustable seats positioned for an average occupant. Refer to the Loading Arrangements diagram for forward and aft limits of occupant CG range.

2. Engine Oil: 8 qt = 15 lb at −0.2 Moment/1,000

Note: The empty weight of this airplane does not include the weight of the oil.

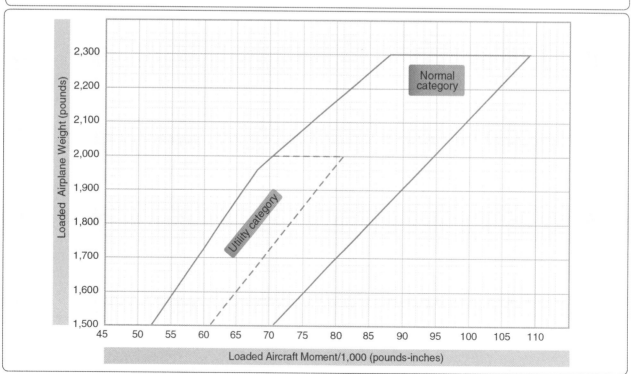

Figure 34. – Airplane Weight and Balance Graphs.

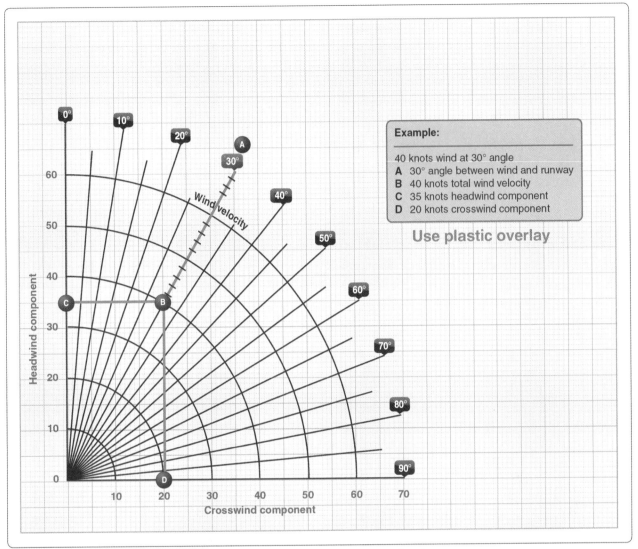

Figure 36. – Crosswind Component Graph.

Gross weight lb	Approach speed, IAS, MPH	Landing distance								Flaps lowered to 40° – Power off Hard surface runway – Zero wind	
		At sea level & 59 °F		At 2,500 feet & 50 °F		At 5,000 feet & 41 °F		At 7,500 feet & 32 °F			
		Ground roll	Total to clear 50 feet OBS	Ground roll	Total to clear 50 feet OBS	Ground roll	Total to clear 50 feet OBS	Ground roll	Total to clear 50 feet OBS		
1,600	60	445	1,075	470	1,135	495	1,195	520	1,255		

NOTE:
1. Decrease the distances shown by 10% for each 4 knots of headwind.
2. Increase the distance by 10% for each 60 °F temperature increase above standard.
3. For operation on a dry, grass runway, increase distance (both "ground roll" and "total to clear 50 feet obstacle") by 20% of the "total to clear 50 feet obstacle" figure.

Figure 38. – Airplane Landing Distance Table.

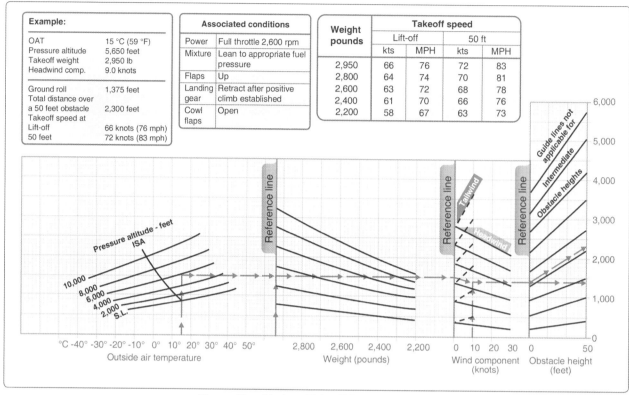

Example:			Associated conditions		Weight pounds	Takeoff speed			
						Lift-off		50 ft	
						kts	MPH	kts	MPH
OAT	15 °C (59 °F)	Power	Full throttle 2,600 rpm		2,950	66	76	72	83
Pressure altitude	5,650 feet	Mixture	Lean to appropriate fuel pressure		2,800	64	74	70	81
Takeoff weight	2,950 lb	Flaps	Up		2,600	63	72	68	78
Headwind comp.	9.0 knots	Landing gear	Retract after positive climb established		2,400	61	70	66	76
Ground roll	1,375 feet	Cowl flaps	Open		2,200	58	67	63	73
Total distance over a 50 feet obstacle	2,300 feet								
Takeoff speed at Lift-off	66 knots (76 mph)								
50 feet	72 knots (83 mph)								

Figure 40. – Airplane Takeoff Distance Graph.

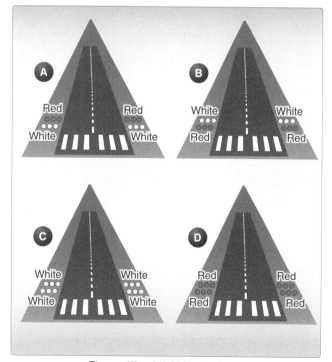

Figure 47. – VASI Illustrations.

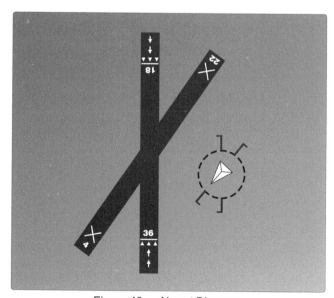

Figure 49. – Airport Diagram.

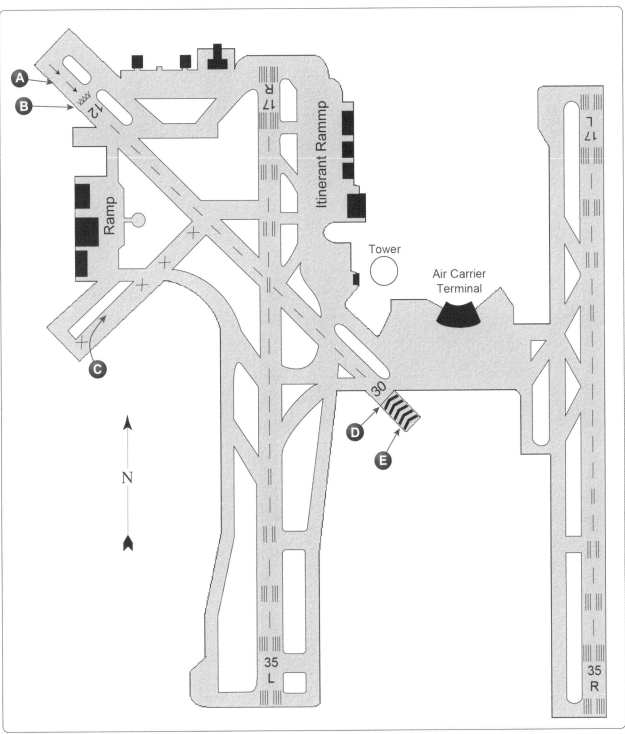

Figure 48. – Airport Diagram.

LINCOLN (LNK)   4 NW   UTC−6(−5DT)   N40°51.05′ W96°45.55′   OMAHA
  1219   B   S4   **FUEL** 100LL, JET A   TPA—See Remarks   ARFF Index—See Remarks   H−5C, L−10I
    NOTAM FILE LNK   IAP, AD 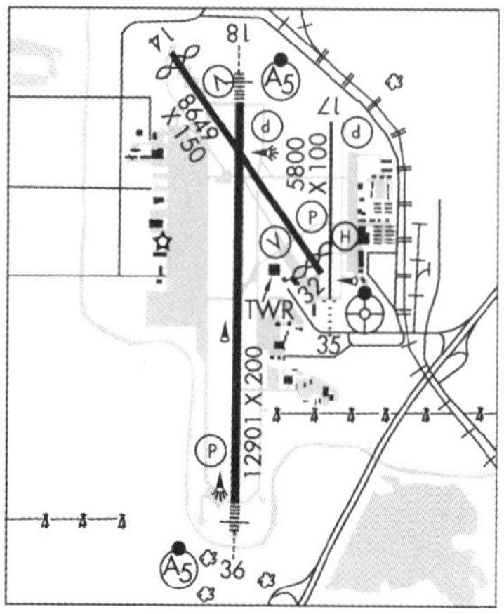
  RWY 18−36: H12901X200 (ASPH−CONC−GRVD)   S−100, D−200,
    2S−175, 2D−400   HIRL
    RWY 18: MALSR. PAPI(P4L)—GA 3.0° TCH 55′. Rgt tfc.   0.4%
      down.
    RWY 36: MALSR. PAPI(P4L)—GA 3.0° TCH 57′.
  RWY 14−32: H8649X150 (ASPH−CONC−GRVD)   S−80, D−170,
    2S−175, 2D−280   MIRL
    RWY 14: REIL. VASI(V4L)—GA 3.0° TCH 48′. Thld dsplcd 363′.
    RWY 32: VASI(V4L)—GA 3.0° TCH 50′. Thld dsplcd 470′.
      Pole.   0.3% up.
  RWY 17−35: H5800X100 (ASPH−CONC−AFSC)   S−49, D−60
    HIRL   0.8% up S
    RWY 17: REIL. PAPI(P4L)—GA 3.0° TCH 44′.
    RWY 35: ODALS. PAPI(P4L)—GA 3.0° TCH 30′. Rgt tfc.
  RUNWAY DECLARED DISTANCE INFORMATION
    RWY 14: TORA−8649 TODA−8649 ASDA−8649 LDA−8286
    RWY 17: TORA−5800 TODA−5800 ASDA−5400 LDA−5400
    RWY 18: TORA−12901 TODA−12901 ASDA−12901 LDA−12901
    RWY 32: TORA−8649 TODA−8649 ASDA−8286 LDA−7816
    RWY 35: TORA−5800 TODA−5800 ASDA−5800 LDA−5800
    RWY 36: TORA−12901 TODA−12901 ASDA−12901 LDA−12901
  AIRPORT REMARKS: Attended continuously. Birds invof arpt. Rwy 18 designated calm wind rwy. Rwy 32 apch holdline
    on South A twy. TPA−2219 (1000), heavy military jet 3000 (1781). Class I, ARFF Index B. ARFF Index C level
    equipment provided. Rwy 18−36 touchdown and rollout rwy visual range avbl. When twr clsd MIRL Rwy 14−32
    preset on low ints, HIRL Rwy 18−36 and Rwy 17−35 preset on med ints, ODALS Rwy 35 operate continuously on
    med ints, MALSR Rwy 18 and Rwy 36 operate continuously and REIL Rwy 14 and Rwy 17 operate continuously
    on low ints. VASI Rwy 14 and Rwy 32, PAPI Rwy 17, Rwy 35, Rwy 18 and Rwy 36 on continuously.
  WEATHER DATA SOURCES: ASOS (402) 474−9214. LLWAS
  COMMUNICATIONS: CTAF 118.5   **ATIS** 118.05   **UNICOM** 122.95
    RCO 122.65 (COLUMBUS RADIO)
  ℝ **APP/DEP CON** 124.0 (180°−359°) 124.8 (360°−179°)
    TOWER 118.5 125.7 (1130−0600Z‡)   **GND CON** 121.9   **CLNC DEL** 120.7
  AIRSPACE: CLASS C svc 1130−0600Z‡ ctc **APP CON** other times **CLASS E.**
  RADIO AIDS TO NAVIGATION: NOTAM FILE LNK.
    (H) VORTACW 116.1   LNK   Chan 108   N40°55.43′ W96°44.52′   181° 4.4 NM to fld. 1370/9E
    POTTS NDB (MHW/LOM) 385   LN   N40°44.83′ W96°45.75′   355° 6.2 NM to fld. Unmonitored when twr clsd.
    ILS 111.1   I−OCZ   Rwy 18.   Class IB   OM unmonitored.
    ILS 109.9   I−LNK   Rwy 36   Class IA   LOM POTTS NDB. MM unmonitored. LOM unmonitored when twr
      clsd.
  COMM/NAV/WEATHER REMARKS: Emerg frequency 121.5 not available at twr.

LOUP CITY MUNI (ØF4)   1 NW   UTC−6(−5DT)   N41°17.20′ W98°59.41′   OMAHA
  2071   B   **FUEL** 100LL   NOTAM FILE OLU   L−10H, 12H
  RWY 16−34: H3200X60 (CONC)   S−12.5   MIRL
    RWY 34: Trees.
  RWY 04−22: 2040X100 (TURF)
    RWY 04: Tree.   **RWY 22:** Road.
  AIRPORT REMARKS: Unattended. For svc call 308−745−1344/1244/0664.
  COMMUNICATIONS: CTAF 122.9
  RADIO AIDS TO NAVIGATION: NOTAM FILE OLU.
    WOLBACH (H) VORTAC 114.8   OBH   Chan 95   N41°22.54′ W98°21.22′   253° 29.3 NM to fld. 2010/7E.

MARTIN FLD   (See SO SIOUX CITY)

Figure 52. – Chart Supplement.

ENROLLMENT CERTIFICATE ✈

This is to certify that

_____

is enrolled in the

Federal Aviation Administration

approved Private Pilot Certification Course

conducted by _____
(name of school and certificate number)

_____
Chief Instructor

_____
Date of Enrollment

GLEIM ®
Aviation

Gleim Publications, Inc.
PO Box 12848
Gainesville, Florida 32604
(800) 874-5346
(352) 375-0772
(352) 375-6940 FAX
GleimAviation.com
aviationteam@gleim.com

GRADUATION CERTIFICATE ✈

This is to certify that

_____

has satisfactorily completed all stages, tests, and
course requirements and has graduated from the
FEDERAL AVIATION ADMINISTRATION
approved Private Pilot Certification Course

conducted by _____
(name of school and certificate number)

The graduate has received _____ hours of cross-country training.

_____
Chief Instructor

_____
Date of Graduation

GLEIM®
Aviation

Gleim Publications, Inc.
PO Box 12848
Gainesville, Florida 32604
(800) 874-5346
(352) 375-0772
(352) 375-6940 FAX
GleimAviation.com
aviationteam@gleim.com

INTRODUCTORY FLIGHT LOG SHEET

If you take one or more introductory flights to help you select the flight school at which you will be most comfortable, have the instructor record your flight time below. If you already have a logbook, be sure to have your instructor record the flight time in it and sign the entry as well.

1. Date: _____ Airplane Make and Model: _____ N-number: _____

   To/From: _____ Total Flight Training Time: _____

Comments:

_____   _____   _____
Instructor Signature   Instructor Cert. No.   Exp. Date

2. Date: _____ Airplane Make and Model: _____ N-number: _____

   To/From: _____ Total Flight Training Time: _____

Comments:

_____   _____   _____
Instructor Signature   Instructor Cert. No.   Exp. Date

3. Date: _____ Airplane Make and Model: _____ N-number: _____

   To/From: _____ Total Flight Training Time: _____

Comments:

_____   _____   _____
Instructor Signature   Instructor Cert. No.   Exp. Date